"*Helping Our Children Grow in Faith* offers a thoughtful, accessible, and practical introduction to the basic building blocks of effective ministries with children. Robert J. Keeley takes seriously children and their spiritual development, challenging congregations to move beyond simplistic approaches that don't fully engage children. In the process, he invites leaders to transform congregations to become communities where children are included, loved, valued, and nurtured by a whole community of caring Christians."

—Eugene C. Roehlkepartain, co-director, Center for Spiritual Development in Childhood and Adolescence Search Institute, Minneapolis, Minnesota

"Drawing on his rich experience as a Children's Ministry Director, Dr. Keeley offers practical suggestions for welcoming children into the faith community as authentic participants. He envisions church as a 'child-friendly culture,' an environment healthy for the spiritual growth of children. And he points the way to forming such a community."

—Cathy Stonehouse, dean, School of Practical Theology and Orlean Bullard Beeson Professor of Christian Discipleship, Asbury Theological Seminary

"I loved this book! Robert Keeley points us in the right direction for building a ministry strategy with children. It is a delight to find someone with a clear vision of how the entire life of the church needs to be developed if we want our children to have a healthy, growing faith in Jesus Christ. This is a 'must read' for every children's pastor and lay leader who cares about the spiritual nurture of children."

—Dr. Kevin E. Lawson, director, PhD and EdD programs in Educational Studies, Talbot School of Theology; editor, *Christian Education Journal*

"'Biblical,' 'practical,' and 'scholarly' is one way to describe Robert J. Keeley's book. 'Warm,' 'gentle,' and 'encouraging' are another set of descriptors. *Helping Our Children Grow in Faith* weaves personal experience with scholarly research and biblical perspectives in offering pastors, parents, and church educators practical wisdom while gently challenging them to consider new ways to offer children a rich, vibrant faith."

—George Brown, Jr., Haworth Professor of Christian Education; associate dean, Western Theological Seminary

"*Helping Our Children Grow in Faith* is an engaging look at the opportunities and challenges of nurturing children's faith. Professor Keeley's clear explanation of faith nurture and thoughtful examination of the role of parents and congregations in the process is a refreshing invitation for the church to reprioritize its children's ministry."

—Darwin Glassford, associate professor of church education; director of MA Programs, Calvin Theological Seminary

"*Helping Our Children Grow in Faith* is an excellent resource for shoring up children's growth in faith. It also is an entry point for exploring the burgeoning field of resources available that address the faith and spiritual life of children."

—Scottie May, professor, Department of Christian Formation and Ministry, Wheaton College

"Keeley has done us all a great service and made very insightful material available. I've always wanted our children to grow in faith, and I've worked hard at it. But now I understand better how it happens, what it takes, and how one stage is different from another. Growing their faith won't happen without growing a church in which they can grow. This book will take you inside the church by taking you inside the process of forming a child's faith!"

—Howard Vanderwell, resource development specialist, Calvin Institute of Christian Worship

"Robert Keeley combines biblical grounding, educational research, and much experience to create this down-to-earth guide. Readers will find here not only practical advice but also a wise proposal about changing our congregational cultures in ways that benefit young and old."

—Debra Rienstra, associate professor of English, Calvin College

"Though this book includes lots of specific 'we could do that' ideas, it is mainly a sweeping vision book. I'd buy it for a parent or committee member who is new to children's ministry or for one who has 'done it all' and needs to remember what it's all about."

—Carolyn Brown, children's ministry consultant and author

"Robert Keeley masterfully describes some of the best current ideas for nurturing children's spiritual development—intentional intergenerationality, the significance of story, the role of wonder—and illustrates them with colorful family stories and incisive vignettes from a variety of church settings."

—Holly Allen, associate professor of Christian Ministries; director, Children and Family Ministries, John Brown University

HeLPING OuR CHiLDReN
GROW IN
FAITH

How the Church Can Nurture the Spiritual Development of Kids

ROBERT J. KEELEY

BakerBooks

Grand Rapids, Michigan

© 2008 by Robert J. Keeley

Published by Baker Books
a division of Baker Publishing Group
P.O. Box 6287, Grand Rapids, MI 49516-6287
www.bakerbooks.com

Printed in the United States of America

Library of Congress Cataloging-in-Publication Data
Keeley, Robert J., 1954–
    Helping our children grow in faith : how the church can nurture the spiritual development of kids / Robert J. Keeley.
        p.   cm.
    Includes bibliographical references.
    ISBN 978-0-8010-6829-4 (pbk.)
    1. Church work with children. 2. Christian education of children. I. Title.
BV639.C4K38 2008
268′.432—dc22   2007028369

In keeping with biblical principles of creation stewardship, Baker Publishing Group advocates the responsible use of our natural resources. As a member of the Green Press Initiative, our company uses recycled paper when possible. The text paper of this book is comprised of 30% post-consumer waste.

Contents

117743

Acknowledgments

I am grateful to many people for their support and help as I wrote this book. I am grateful to my colleagues at Calvin College, specifically to the faculty and staff of the Education Department. They have supported my work, and I appreciate them as colleagues and friends. Thanks also to Gloria Stronks, a former colleague, who read an early draft of the manuscript and made a number of helpful comments.

The Calvin Institute of Christian Worship and its director John Witvliet have encouraged me to continue to work out the ideas presented in this book and have given me a number of opportunities to talk with people in the field and to present these ideas. Kristen VerHulst, Kathy Smith, and Joyce Borger were helpful in making comments on an early draft of this manuscript. Summer 2005 Seminar in Christian Scholarship group led by John Witvliet also read and discussed this work, making valuable comments.

My friends Ron and Debra Rienstra were encouraging throughout the process of writing this book. The discussions that Laura and I had with them about these topics were illuminating and fun. Ron was often my go-to guy on matters of theology, and he was always helpful and patient with me as I tried out new ideas.

I have been greatly blessed through the churches that I have been a member of throughout my life. Most recently Pastor Marv Hofman and the congregation at Fourteenth Street Christian Reformed Church, where Laura and I serve as Children's Ministry Directors, have been helpful in giving us many positive examples of what it means to welcome children into the full fellowship of the church. The children we have been blessed to work with there have ministered to me as much as I have to them.

My parents, John and Ratie Keeley, and my in-laws, Gerald and Marjorie VanderKooy, have given me concrete examples of how to raise children who know and love the Lord.

This book would not have happened had I not been a partner in life and in ministry with my wife, Laura. She has been my best friend and my most ardent fan and critic for over thirty years. We talk about ministry to children together almost daily. Aside from collaborating in ministry and in writing, we also have four children: Bethany, Meredith, Bryan, and Lynnae. I'm richly blessed to be their father.

Thanks be to God.

Robert Keeley

1

Three-Dimensional Faith

A few years ago my eighty-three-year-old father-in-law fell and broke his hip. He had been slipping a bit mentally over the previous year or so, and we were starting to be concerned about him. After the surgery to repair his hip, he went to a nursing home so he could get the care he needed. Soon after he arrived there, we noticed a sharp decrease in his mental abilities. There were a number of things he seemed unable to understand. He would try to get up and walk, for example, forgetting that he wasn't yet able to do that. And there were times when he did not recognize us. Also he didn't seem to grasp why he had to stay at the nursing home. He wanted to go home and asked anyone and everyone to help him get out of that place.

As my wife and I were discussing this at the dinner table one evening, Lynnae, our twelve-year-old daughter, asked a question: "What if Grandpa forgets about God?" Lynnae was grappling with a pretty good theological question. At a fairly young age she was concerned about one of the very core issues of faith.

In this case, I had an answer to Lynnae's question: "Even if Grandpa forgets about God, God won't forget about Grandpa."

My point is not that I know all of the answers to life's questions, because I don't—despite my occasional attempts to convince my children that I do. The point is that Lynnae, as well as many children, thinks deeply about spiritual issues.

It isn't just children who grow up in the church who have questions about God. A few years ago, Tricia, a seven-year-old, who was a neighbor of one of our church families, hung around their house so much that they would often have to shoo her away when the family was going somewhere. One Sunday morning, instead of telling Tricia that she'd have to go home, our friends asked if she would like to go to church with them. She went along and found something there that resonated with her. She became a regular fixture at our church that year and for a few years after that, involved in church school, children's worship, and potluck dinners. Tricia was at most church events, sometimes having to find a ride to get there and occasionally even dragging her mom along with her. Soon she became a member of our church. It seemed pretty clear that the Holy Spirit had been working in Tricia's heart long before our church came on the scene for her.

There are lots of stories like this and lots of churches that have been homes to children like Tricia and Lynnae. Often the Holy Spirit works in children's hearts without our help, as he did in Tricia's, but he also used her neighbors and other members of our church to help her come to know God personally.

Lynnae had quite a different story. She grew up in a home with parents who loved the Lord and who talked to her about God and took her to church. Both girls, though, had spiritual questions, indicating that they have profound thoughts about the things of God. As parents and church educators, we want to make sure that children like Lynnae and Tricia have the opportunity to meet God no matter what their faith background. We want them to grow in a way that allows them to build a strong faith, a faith that remains firm throughout their life.

God's Work or Ours?

So if we want to encourage faith in children, what do we do? Is faith mostly a "God thing," or can we have a real impact on the beliefs of children? Faith comes from God. Any fancy curriculum or great words on our part or the part of any teacher or adult can't change the fact that the Holy Spirit has to work in the hearts of people to move them toward God. We don't have to wait for a particular moment to ask children to accept the Lord nor do we have to worry about missing the one chance we might have to tell our children about faith. God is in charge of them and the Holy Spirit works in their hearts to bring them to him.

But here's another thing that is also true: the things we do with children to build their faith are very important. They are so important, in fact, that God chooses to use our actions and words to impact the way some people understand who he is and how they can live to serve him. There are times when, as a teacher, I haven't been particularly inspirational and my teaching has been far from excellent, but I believe that God has been able to use my teaching to touch the hearts of children and young people anyway, even when I did it poorly.

As I grew up, some of my church school teachers were not very good. I'm not sure I thought much about it at the time but looking back it is easy for me to see that some of those classes weren't run very well. And this is true of many Sunday school teachers; most aren't great. In many churches the vast majority of adults who teach are untrained. Some of them are good natural teachers but others just simply love the Lord and love kids. But here's the amazing thing: a number of those teachers and leaders helped me learn a lot about God and what it means to live my life as a Christian, even though they didn't "do it right." In fact, looking back on how I came to know the Lord, it is hard for me to sort out any one particular person or moment when God's presence in my life became real to me. The way that I came to know him was more of a tapestry, a weaving together of the things that I learned from many people in many places. Each person was important, because each of them had a role to play in helping me understand God and his place in my life. I'm grateful to God for all of them.

We know that the Holy Spirit moves the hearts of people toward God; we don't. Yet God uses people in the process. It doesn't seem possible that these two things can both be true, but I believe they are. Jesus told his disciples: "Go into all the world and preach the good news to all creation" (Mark 16:15). Jesus's words call us to preach the Good News to *all of creation*— including children. God has planned for us to play a part in helping children know who he is. So when children come with questions—like Lynnae did about her grandfather or Tricia did about who God is—we have a responsibility to answer these questions well.

A Simple and Complex Faith

Marva Dawn is among those who argue that this is a particularly important time for those of us involved in ministry to children.[1] She points out that the level of biblical literacy for most people in U.S. society has dropped. She cites personal experience at a Christian college where eleven out of twelve religion majors didn't know the story of Gideon and the fleece. Whether this is a result of the advent of post-modernism, as she suggests, or if there are other causes, the result is that we seem to have raised a generation of young people who do not know the Bible and don't have a church background.[2] The need for people other than parents to have a role in nurturing the faith of young people has perhaps never been greater.

When we talk to children about faith, we need to explain things in clear and simple terms, even though theological ideas can be very complex. However, our faith *is* very simple. Karl Barth, the great theologian, summarized his greatest theological insight with these words: "Jesus loves me; this I know, for the Bible tells me so."[3] It doesn't get much simpler than that. Our stereotype of children's faith is that it is just as simple as that famous children's song indicates, but as Lynnae's question reveals, children can have complex questions concerning faith.

Children who live in difficult circumstances can have deep questions about their faith. Children who have been abused, for example, or children whose parents have divorced can ask very difficult questions, and we want to be able to give them good answers. We want these children to know that we have a solid faith, a faith that is dependable when things are not easy, because our God is dependable. We also want them to know that we have a faith that is rich enough and deep enough to entertain difficult questions.

The tougher the question, though, the more difficult it is to articulate a simple answer. So we have an interesting dilemma. How do we explain our faith to children in ways that are simple enough for children to understand, but, at the same time, how do we help them develop a deep faith that is able to stand up to the questions that they will ask? We want to help children build a faith that has three dimensions, a faith that affects their head, their heart, and their spirit. We want our children to know God and love God, and we want God to be an important part of the fabric of their lives.

The stories of faith in the Bible reveal who God is and how he works in people's lives. As such they are the basis for our faith and for the faith of our children. These stories form the bedrock of a faith that endures regardless of what life is like. It is a faith that is built on a firm foundation of true and reasonable belief. Those who have a three-dimensional faith know what they believe and who God is and what he said.

It is not enough just to know what we believe. Our children need to know God. They need to have a relationship with him. A three-dimensional faith is more than just head knowledge; the heart must also be involved. Our children must learn to love God and to love each other, not with a sappy Valentine's Day love, but with an emotion that runs deep and shows a commitment to others that does not fade. Children can rejoice with friends and family over God's blessings and grieve with each other's sorrows, bringing their grief to God. If their hearts are attuned to his heart, they will be able to share with God all that they are and all that they experience.

Our children's faith, and our own, should be part of the very fabric of their lives, so much a part of them that it comes out in their language and their thoughts, even when they aren't talking about religion. Their faith should not be like a bumper sticker; it should be part of their DNA. A three-dimensional faith is a faith that is rooted deep inside so that even when our head doubts or our heart falters, our faith remains strong. This faith goes beyond platitudes and catchphrases. It's a faith that realizes that God is faithful even when our questions go unanswered.

Building Strong Faith

Recently we have witnessed the destructive power of hurricanes as they have battered the Gulf States. The force of the wind has torn apart buildings and homes, tossed them about, and discarded them. I remember one woman in Florida who was evacuated from her home, but she felt her house would be secure because it had been built to hurricane specifications. She believed it would withstand the storm better than the older homes that weren't as strong.

Like homes built to hurricane specifications, a three-dimensional faith is strong enough to withstand the storms of life without buckling under the pressure. Helping children develop this kind of faith is a long-term task, one that isn't accomplished through flashy programs or high-powered special events.

No program can take the place of a mentoring relationship between an older Christian man or woman and a child who is learning to love the Lord. Children develop a three-dimensional faith by walking alongside older brothers and sisters in Christ who share the rich stories of faith found in the Bible, who listen when hard questions come up, and who take the time to talk through appropriate responses to these questions.

Of course church programs and spiritual presentations aren't bad. Programs that help adults find ways to connect with children in a systematic way can be beneficial and do not work against the personal mentoring that is being suggested here. Before we can develop programs that are successful in building strong faith in children, though, we must know God's Word, grasp what God says about children, and understand how children develop.

Know God's Word

We meet God in his Word, so we need to hear and read it often until Scripture becomes a part of us. If the stories of the

Bible are part of who we are, they affect how we think about the world and about situations in our lives. The story of Esther, for example, is one that I think about when I wonder if I can serve God in some particular setting. Esther found herself in Persia serving as the queen of a foreign people and was called on to put her life on the line to save the Hebrews. If Esther was called to serve God in that setting, then can there be any place where God can't use me?

When I can't see where God is leading me, I sometimes think about Joseph. Joseph didn't know God's plan when his brothers threw him in a pit and sold him into slavery. He couldn't see the end of the story, how he would end up in the king's service, saving thousands of people from a famine, including his own family. He saw none of that when he was waiting in the pit. All he could see was the blackness of his situation. When I can't see how God could use a situation that I find myself in, I sometimes remember that Joseph couldn't see the end of his story either.

David, a man after God's own heart, struggled with adultery and with being a poor parent. The story of David and Bathsheba provokes many questions. Did Bathsheba know what she was doing when she took a bath next door to the palace? Certainly David knew better than to get involved with her, but he let his emotions, not his good sense, drive his actions. Even after David's adultery and his murder of Bathsheba's husband, David and Bathsheba's child, Solomon, the future king of Israel, was a man of great wisdom.

David did not have good relationships with his children. His son Absalom wanted to kill him and take over the throne. When Absalom was killed in the revolt, David was overcome with grief. One of his generals had to tell him to quit his over-the-top grieving and put on a good face for all the soldiers who had risked their lives to defend him from the rebellion.

Despite David's weaknesses, God saw fit to use him. Not only that, but David is revered in the pages of Scripture and in the history of the Jewish people. If God can make heroes out of people like David, then God can use me too, despite my flaws. It is good for me to have these stories in mind as I encounter different challenges in my life. They help me see that God is with me and that I can trust him to be faithful even when I am not.

One of the amazing things about the Bible is that a person can read it, and, with no other help, discover who God is and come to a saving knowledge of Jesus Christ. The Bible is such a rich and wonderful book that we can always learn more from it about God and about who we are. Using commentaries, archeological studies, and historical books will bring a deeper and richer view of the time and the place in which biblical stories were written. We can learn to see the people in these stories as real people and their experiences as real events. This understanding is an important part of our preparation for ministry to young people, for if we are to bring God's Word as a living, breathing document to children, we need to know it.

Know Children

To minister to children, we must understand them, their special needs, and their abilities. We can learn about children in the Bible. There are some passages in which children play a role and others where Jesus actually talks about children. The Bible, however, was not written as a textbook on child development, so we also need to take a look at what psychologists and educators say about children. Much has been written about the way children learn and how they think. Theories of cognitive development explain how the ability to think grows and changes as children get older. We also need to grasp how children change emotionally, socially, and morally as they mature. John Westerhoff and James Fowler are two theorists who have studied faith development, and their findings can aid our understanding. Looking at how children grow will give us additional clues about how we can and should design ministry for children that supports the development of a three-dimensional faith.

Six Principles

There are six principles that are important in ministry to children, which we'll be looking at throughout this book.

1. Children need to be nurtured in their faith by the whole community of faith, not just their parents.
2. Children need to be part of the whole life of the church.
3. Children need to know that God is mysterious.
4. Bible stories are the key to helping children know a God who is mysterious and who knows them for who they are.
5. Faith and moral development are both important but they are not the same thing.
6. Children should be part of congregational worship and they should also have opportunities to experience developmentally appropriate worship.

By looking at these six principles we will develop ideas that will be useful as we try to offer experiences to children in our churches and homes that will help them build the kind of three-dimensional faith that we want them to have. Spending time with children in mentoring relationships may determine how they grow in faith.

The Holy Spirit is working in the lives of children, and God calls us to be part of that work. The questions children ask reveal their thirst for a deep knowledge of God that will not be satisfied in the long term with shallow answers. If we really want to help children grow in faith, we need to do all we can to use the tools that God has given us.

It's a wonderful task. Let's get started.

2

The Church as Community

Principle 1: Children need to be nurtured in their faith by the whole community of faith, not just their parents.

One of the joys I have in my church is that I get to present candles to families at infant baptism. While holding the lit candle, I usually speak briefly about some passage of Scripture or some Bible story and connect it to our church's understanding of covenant.

One Sunday I was planning to use the story of Jesus at the temple as a young boy. In the car on the way to church, one of our children (my wife and I have four) asked what I was going to talk about. I mentioned the story of Jesus in the temple and said that I was going to cite it as an example of how the Bible can be used as a parenting manual.

My son Bryan, who was seventeen at the time, laughed and said, "So you're going to tell them to let their kids go anywhere they want without telling their parents? Cool!"

We got a good laugh out of it, and that conversation found its way into my morning talk, because my point was that parents who read the Bible looking for tips on how to raise their children are not going to find many. The only story in which we get a glimpse of Jesus's parents doing any parenting is the one about Jesus being left alone in the temple. The Bible is not meant to be a parenting guidebook. In fact there is no family in the Bible that seems to be a model for a modern Christian family. This can be frustrating for parents as they look at Cain and Abel, Jacob and Esau, and other siblings and see that the Bible is filled with families in crisis, and sometimes it seems that these crises are a direct result of poor parenting. Does this mean that we can learn nothing about raising children from the Bible? Not quite.

The Family in First-Century Israel

From reading the Bible, it appears that Jesus's parents followed Jewish traditions quite carefully. For example, we know that they presented baby Jesus in the temple after the time of Mary's purification was complete (Luke 2:22–23). We also know that they celebrated the Jewish feast of Passover by going to Jerusalem and that they took Jesus along. Here's what we read in Luke 2:41–50:

> Every year his parents went to Jerusalem for the Feast of the Passover. When he was twelve years old, they went up to the Feast, according to the custom. After the Feast was over, while his parents were returning home, the boy Jesus stayed behind in Jerusalem, but they were unaware of it. Thinking he was in their company, they traveled on for a day. Then they began looking for him among their relatives and friends. When they did not find him, they went back to Jerusalem to look for him. After three days they found him in the temple courts, sitting among

the teachers, listening to them and asking them questions. Everyone who heard him was amazed at his understanding and his answers. When his parents saw him, they were astonished. His mother said to him, "Son, why have you treated us like this? Your father and I have been anxiously searching for you."

"Why were you searching for me?" he asked. "Didn't you know I had to be in my Father's house?" But they did not understand what he was saying to them.

To understand this passage it is helpful to look at the Jewish notion of family that was in effect at this time. The Hebrew word that is used for family is *mishpahah*.[1] To translate this word merely as "family," though, does not really do it justice. The family unit in Israel was more complex and tightly knit than most modern North American families.[2] In a very real sense, all of Israel considered themselves one family, since they all thought of themselves as children of Abraham. Their personal identity was also determined partly by their tribe, based on which of the children of Jacob was their most direct male ancestor. Allegiance to the tribe was only part of the system, however. There were smaller groups or clans to which family groups belonged and from which wives were chosen.

All of this formed an overarching layer to the actual nuclear family that existed at the time. The nuclear family was different than it is now. Today a family generally consists of parents and children, two generations living together. Grandparents living with their children is more an exception than it is a rule, at least in North America. In first-century Israel, though, people typically lived in what they called "their father's house"—the house that was owned by their oldest living male ancestor.[3] This house often had three or four generations of people living together.[4] A man's sons, grandsons, and often great-grandsons, along with their wives and their servants all lived together in a house. Actually, this house was more like a compound—almost a small village with several separate structures. This patriarchal system placed a number of responsibilities on the father of the household. One of these responsibilities was to lead the family in the celebration of national festivals, such as Passover.[5]

We are not told who took the trip with Mary, Joseph, and Jesus to Jerusalem, but we do know that the couple went with a pretty large group and, given the way things were at that time, the group was probably their family—the kind who all lived together in their "father's house." An interesting thing takes place on Mary and Joseph's return trip. Apparently they traveled for an entire day before starting to search for Jesus. I don't think that Mary and Joseph were negligent in their care for young Jesus. Rather, they assumed that Jesus was with relatives in the large group. This is not negligence; this is just the way things were—the community cared for the children.

It Takes a Community

The idea of a community sharing responsibility for the raising of children has real merit. In his book on the Jewish roots of Christianity, Marvin Wilson writes about the family structure of first-century Israel. He ends his section on the support of the community by writing: "No one is strong enough to make it through life alone. Everyone needs support."[6] The Jewish concept of the family reminds us in many ways that the extended community of faith is crucial for the health and strength of today's church and home.

Raising children may be one of the most important tasks we do as individuals and as a community. Doing it alone is difficult at best and sometimes nearly impossible. It needs to be done with the support of a community. Unfortunately, our twenty-first-century social structures work against us. At this time in history the family structure that we have in North America is a far cry from that of first-century Israel. Jesus's parents had the support of his uncles, aunts, grandparents, and maybe even great-grandparents, but today we often find family members living quite far from each other. People move much more than they did even one generation ago. Technology allows us to stay in touch, but grandparents sending emails to their grandchildren is not at all the same thing as talking with them and taking care of them. Our work schedules have changed and so our jobs often keep us away from extended family even if we live near each other. We may see our families on holidays or for a week or so of vacation each year but certainly not often enough for the kind of mutual support that Jesus's parents experienced.

There are other recent indications that this lack of extended family is having a negative impact on our children. The Commission for Children at Risk published a report in which they wrote: "Large and growing numbers of U.S. children are suffering from mental illness, emotional distress and behavioral problems."[7] They suggest that the cause for these problems is a lack of connectedness to people and to moral and spiritual meaning. In the past this connectedness came through social institutions, but today these institutions are deteriorating. The commission says that there is scientific evidence that people are "hardwired for close attachments to other people, beginning with our mothers, fathers, and extended family, and then moving out to the broader community."[8]

The spiritual life of the family in first-century Israel was not limited to the small nuclear family unit as we see it today. The festivals reminding the people of God's faithfulness were national affairs and their celebrations were community events. Both Jesus's family and the larger community took responsibility for his spiritual development. We need to find ways to achieve some of the sense of community and family that Jesus and others of that era experienced.

The Commission for Children at Risk makes the case for "authoritative communities." This commission does not specify what these communities might be but gives us a description of what they are like (see the sidebar). We can see that the list describes what the church ought to be for all of us. Living as a church community provides a wonderful opportunity to lift each other up in our roles as parents and as brothers and sisters in Christ. We have an opportunity to give the children in our church the kind of support they need. Our churches can be *mishpahah* for our children, following the Jewish idea that family includes the broader community. But it can only be *mishpahah* if we are deliberate and thoughtful about the way we do ministry for and with parents.

What Is an Authoritative Community?

1. It is a social institution that includes children and youth.
2. It treats children as ends in themselves.
3. It is warm and nurturing—rules matter, but so do closer relationships.
4. It establishes clear limits and expectations—close relationships matter, but so do rules and expectations.
5. The core of its work is performed largely by nonspecialists.
6. It is multi-generational—children benefit enormously from being around people in all stages of the life cycle.
7. It has a long-term focus.
8. It reflects and transmits a shared understanding of what it means to be a good person.
9. It encourages spiritual and religious development.
10. It is philosophically oriented to the equal dignity of all persons and the principle of love of neighbor.

Hardwired to Connect: The New Scientific Case for Authoritative Communities, 34

Making Church a House of Learning

The Jewish culture had a system of education that helped ensure that all children learned the Torah, the book of the law, what we know as the first books of the Old Testament. By their early teen years all children attended the *bet talmud*, the "house of learning." At age thirteen, students who were especially gifted attended the *bet midrash*, the "house of study."[9] The Gospel writer points out that Jesus was twelve years old at the time of the story in Luke, and he would not have been quite old enough to participate in the *bet midrash*. He was old enough, though, for the teacher and his parents to know that he was a candidate for additional learning.

The passage in Luke reminds us that the larger community took responsibility for educating and for raising up children to know who God is. We should do no less.

Much of this sense of community comes from caring for each other as brothers and sisters in Christ. Sometimes, though, helping children feel like part of the community takes some extra thought. Three examples of how this can happen come to mind. One young couple I know, Steve and Leanne, were asked to serve as high school youth group leaders in their church. The church knew that Steve and Leanne had three small children who would need to be taken care of while their parents spent time with the teens at church, so the parents of the teens volunteered to take turns spending Sunday evenings with Steve and Leanne's children. This turned out to be a wonderful experience for everyone. Steve and Leanne did a great job with the high school students, and older parents got to know these younger kids a lot better. The kids enjoyed it too. They looked forward to having another couple from church come and listen to their stories and play games with them every other week. The sense of community that was built through this sharing of responsibility for children built up the entire congregation. The high school students got to know Steve and Leanne's children well too, and it was common to find four-year-old Noah in the arms of a high school junior or senior after church on a Sunday morning.

Another youth leader, Maria, volunteered to take her youth group on a weeklong service project, but she also had childcare issues. Her husband would be home in the evenings but he was unable to get off from work to care for their three girls during the day. Again the church stepped up and offered to take the girls, a different family each day. What really made this remarkable, though, is that each day the girls got to do something special—a trip to the zoo or to the botanical gardens, for example. Every day the adults who cared for them took pictures of the special things they did and made a book so they could share their exciting adventures with their parents. Through sharing this responsibility, church families got to know the girls better, the youth group had a great trip, and the girls had a ball. Above all, the sense of community grew in the church as people took corporate responsibility to help care for Maria's children while she cared for their teens.

One more example: a number of years ago our church started a mentoring program for high school students, and I was asked to serve as the mentor for Ben, a young man who was a high school senior. Ben and I got to know each other pretty well that year. We spent time talking together, and we both took a gifts inventory and discussed where we thought we could serve God with our abilities. We visited another church together just to see how they worshiped and we talked about the experience. There wasn't a whole lot of time involved for either of us; we just made sure we kept the connection going and got together as often as we could.

Ben left for college and then got a job that kept him on the road, but even though long periods of time passed when we didn't see each other, we managed to stay in touch. My wife and I were invited to his college graduation party and were thrilled recently to receive an invitation to his wedding. Through the bond we developed, Ben was drawn closer to the church and kept in touch with the community. He wasn't a kid who needed special attention and he didn't have any particular educational needs. His parents were great people who related well to their son. Our connection wasn't meant to take the place of another relationship that was missing. It was just a chance for a young man to get to know an older man in our church, someone else in the community who cared about him and with whom he could share thoughts about growing as a Christian.

In a sense the word *community* isn't quite rich enough to show the kind of reciprocal caring seen in these examples. The word *family* comes pretty close. In fact there are some things about modern-day families that can help the church understand how to give children the sort of support they received in Jesus's time.[10]

Becoming Family

We don't usually need to convince our children that they are members of our family—they just are. We include them from the moment they are born or adopted. While we treat our children differently when they grow up or as they reach adulthood, we don't make them wait until then to become full members of the family. As a church, however, it seems that we sometimes don't really consider children full members of the body. We see them as *potential* members, people who will be members when they get older.

Ironically, instead of seeing children and teens as current members of the church, sometimes we act as though we need to convince them to become members of the church (targeting them with evangelistic opportunities), while at the same time we don't do the simple things that might be the most valuable in helping them see themselves as part of the family—talking to them about what we do and why. It can be as simple and as profound as telling children our stories—telling them how we have experienced God's working in our lives at various times.

We already tell our children stories. As parents, we tell stories about how we met our spouse, how we got our job, and the births of the kids. In fact sometimes we tell these stories only to our children, as they come up naturally out of conversations we have with them. As parents and fellow church members, we need to speak just as naturally about our faith stories. The stories of faith include the stories of the Bible but they also include our personal faith stories, which we don't often tell our children. The Lord knew that this would be something that parents would need some prodding to do. In Joshua 4:4–7 we read:

> So Joshua called together the twelve men he had appointed from the Israelites, one from each tribe, and said to them, "Go over before the ark of the LORD your God into the middle of the Jordan. Each of you is to take up a stone on his shoulder, according to the number of the tribes of the Israelites, to serve as a sign among you. In the future, when your children ask you, 'What do these stones mean?' tell them that the flow of the Jordan was cut off before the ark of the covenant of the LORD. When it crossed the Jordan, the waters of the Jordan were cut off. These stones are to be a memorial to the people of Israel forever."

Joshua set up a marker so that parents would be asked questions that would remind them to tell the story of God's deliverance. We need to tell our children our stories too.

One way my church encouraged parents to do this was to develop some specific times for it to happen. In our first and second grade worship center,[11] we invited the parents of the children, one each week, to come and be interviewed by the worship leader about their faith and about what things were like for them when they were children.[12] We were thrilled at the response of parents to this idea. One parent brought in the pin that he received as a young boy for attendance in Sunday school. The children had not seen a pin like this, and it allowed the parent to talk with them about his experience in Sunday school and how it set the stage for his faith today. Another parent brought a picture of himself when he was the age of his daughter. He was dressed in his Sunday best and had the same gaping hole in his mouth where his tooth used to be that his daughter had on the day he brought in the picture. This led nicely into a discussion of what has changed and what is the same since those days. It allowed the parent to talk easily about how God does not change.

Not only in Joshua's time but today, parents need reminders to talk with their children and with the other children in church about faith. One of the things we can do in children's ministry is to provide these opportunities and to encourage parents to use them.

In addition to these opportunities to talk directly about faith, however, we need to make sure that children, throughout all their growing-up years, are able to interact with many members of the congregation—both young and old. Recently twenty-two-year-old Anna wrote an open letter to her church in which she reflected on this very thing. The letter was published in the church's monthly newsletter. As she sat at a wedding shower (thrown for her and another young bride by church friends), she was struck by how important her church family had been to her as she was growing up. She wrote that the shower wasn't just a time to give gifts, "this was a group of moms giving their blessing on two young women they had helped raise." She goes on to say, "[The] joint help of parenthood was not limited to the women in that room, but extended to many [of our church's] men and women." As she was stepping out into a new phase of her life, she wanted to express her gratitude to the many people who had given her "and countless other youngsters unlimited love in order to shape me into a child of God."

I'm not sure that Anna's church managed to connect with all (or even most) of the young people the way they did with Anna, but the point is that this is an example of how the church can be the type of family that we read about in the first century. Anna wrote, "The most amazing thing about this joint-parenthood is how little we are all aware of it. The outpouring of love on our children and raising them together with the responsibility of molding them to be men and women of God happens quite naturally and quietly at our church." It happened because people took the time to get to know children and teens as people. It's when we *individually* take the time to get to know the kids in our own church that we can have the most impact on them *collectively*. As a church, though, it is important to try to build a culture in our congregation where this sort of thing can happen. One way to do that is to have an authentic place for our children and teens in the structured life of the church.

Authentic Tasks

Children and young people should participate in the life of the church through authentic tasks. By *authentic* I mean tasks in which they give as well as receive. They should feel that if they aren't doing their part, the whole group will suffer. We do not accomplish this by giving them special places to worship or by setting them aside in their own subgroups. On the contrary, it is these very things that help them see themselves as merely *potential* members of the church. We need to include them in worship and in other parts of the life of the church, doing useful things that they are able to do.

In her book *So Much More: An Invitation to Christian Spirituality*, Debra Reinstra writes about a church that does this well.

> Everyone lingered after worship and mixed together: married people, single people, old people, children, and, most amazingly, teenagers. In my opinion, teenagers are the canaries in the coal mine of community and I've never seen a church with a more cheerful involved crew of them. If, as in this church, teenagers are obviously known, loved and (not incidentally) needed, if they are integrated into the daily tasks of the community with roles to play and work to do, something is going right. In this church teenagers were considered regular citizens, working in the nursery, playing instruments in worship, and running the sound board. They responded to this integration by accepting the mentoring of older people and also by providing their own capable mentoring of the tiniest members of the church. This cross-generational modeling was the primary active ingredient in the bonding compound that held this church together.[13]

As Reinstra points out, one important way to make children and teens feel like part of the community is to have authentic tasks for them to do. Even if your church does not have official acolytes, consider having an elementary-aged child come in at the beginning of the service and light the candle. In addition to this candlelighting, some churches have another child bring in the Bible, making a point of bringing God's Word into the sanctuary at the beginning of the service and then bringing it out into the world at the end of the service. We have found that giving children the responsibility for doing these tasks has encouraged them to take them seriously. Before church every Sunday, they get themselves ready, get the Bible and candlelighter, and carefully prepare to walk down the center aisle. They are great about waiting for each other in the front of the church if the candlelighting takes a little longer on some Sundays. They have learned that this is a task that requires more ceremony than other things that they do and they are thrilled to have a part in the service.

My wife, Laura, who directs children's ministries with me at our church in Michigan, originally arranged for third graders to carry in the Bible and light the candle. Recently we spoke with Luke, a third grader who was one of the candlelighters. He said that he had looked forward for a long time to being a candlelighter, because he saw children do it when he was younger and knew that his turn would come. He was excited about being able to serve the church in this way.

Luke also knows that when he gets to seventh and eighth grade, he'll be able to do what his older sister does, help in our children's worship centers. These students are given the responsibility to work with younger children and be role models for them as well as assist the teachers in getting materials ready and helping the children as they worship together. These helpers are an important part of our program and when they aren't available, we need to find substitutes. These middle school students know that we need them and they look forward to being asked to participate. In fact, often a number of them want to help, even when they're not scheduled.

In some churches there are a number of high school students who love to work with the sound and video equipment. These students take their work very seriously and, if given the chance, really take ownership of that aspect of church life. They arrive early to set up for worship and they come in during the week to try things out and make things better with the system. They realize they are needed and important in the life of the church and play an important role in enhancing worship. When children and teens are serving the church, they feel like a real part of the body of Christ instead of a group for whom special programs are created until they are old enough to really take part. Don Posterski wrote about the importance of significant participation in his book *Friendship*. His survey research in Canada showed that teenagers felt that adults did not consider their opinions. He wrote that "restricting young people to activities that lack significance is an insult to their abilities."[14]

Giving children and teens the opportunity to make a real contribution to their church is indeed important, but more important than this are the *connections* that they make with the people with whom they interact. Relationships have a more lasting impact than programs. Churches need to work to make sure that our children and teens see their church as the kind of authoritative community that Jesus experienced when he was growing up. In this way we will support their need for family that everyone has and encourage faith by giving them a place in which they feel welcomed and needed. If we want our children to consider their faith a central part of who they are, if we want their faith to go beyond just their minds and hearts, then the community of faith needs to develop a number of ways to connect with young people and children. If we want them to develop a three-dimensional faith, we need to be ready to walk with them.

3

Jesus Values Children

Principle 2: Children need to be part of the whole life of the church.

Jesus didn't talk just to adults. He interacted with children during his ministry years and said things about them that we should consider as we think about our work with children. If we want to help our children have a three-dimensional faith, we ought to take Jesus's words about children very seriously. Did Jesus say or do things with children that can give us a hint about how to help them put their faith at the center of their lives? Let's take a look.

Jesus Heals Children

The first thing we notice is that most of Jesus's interactions with children that are recorded in the Gospels have to do with healing. There are four stories in which Jesus heals children.

Jesus Heals Children

Jesus heals Jairus's daughter—Matthew 9:18–26; Mark 5:21–43; Luke 8:41–56

Jairus, one of the synagogue rulers, asks Jesus to come and heal his daughter. Along the way, Jesus stops when a woman in the crowd touches his garment, and this heals her. Before they can get on their way again, men arrive saying that the little girl is already dead. Jesus tells Jairus, "Don't be afraid; just believe" (Mark 5:36). With that he goes on to Jairus's house and raises the young girl from the dead.

Jesus heals a child in Capernaum—John 4:46–54

A royal official comes to Jesus saying that his son is very sick. Jesus tells him that his son will live and, as the man is returning home, a messenger meets him with the good news that his son is better. The time he began to get better matches the time that Jesus told the official that his son would live.

Jesus heals a boy who has a demon—Matthew 17:14–20; Mark 9:14–29; Luke 9:37–43

A man in the crowd begs Jesus to look at his son who is thrown into convulsions by an evil spirit. The man had asked Jesus's disciples to drive the spirit out of the boy, but they were not able. Jesus sees the boy in the midst of convulsions, rebukes the spirit, and heals the boy.

Jesus heals the daughter of a woman from Phoenicia—Matthew 15:21–28; Mark 7:24–30

A woman from Phoenicia begs Jesus to send an evil spirit out of her daughter. "'First let the children eat all they want,' he told her, 'for it is not right to take the children's bread and toss it to their dogs.' 'Yes, Lord,' she replied, 'but even the dogs under the table eat the children's crumbs.' Then he told her, 'For such a reply, you may go; the demon has left your daughter.' She went home and found her child lying on the bed, and the demon gone" (Mark 7:27–30).

On the surface, there seems to be little that we can learn about Jesus's view of children from these healing events. It does seem clear, though, that Jesus cares about people's physical well-being. He isn't merely concerned with their eternal destiny. He wants children and adults to be whole in body as well as in spirit. Let's look at one of these stories.[1]

> While Jesus was still speaking, someone came from the house of Jairus, the synagogue ruler. "Your daughter is dead," he said. "Don't bother the teacher any more."
>
> Hearing this, Jesus said to Jairus, "Don't be afraid; just believe, and she will be healed."
>
> When he arrived at the house of Jairus, he did not let anyone go in with him except Peter, John and James, and the child's father and mother. Meanwhile, all the people were wailing and mourning for her. "Stop wailing," Jesus said. "She is not dead but asleep."
>
> They laughed at him, knowing that she was dead. But he took her by the hand and said, "My child, get up!" Her spirit returned, and at once she stood up. Then Jesus told them to give her something to eat. Her parents were astonished, but he ordered them not to tell anyone what had happened.
>
> Luke 8:49–56

Passages like this (and other stories of healing) tell us that Jesus places value on children. Jesus went to Jairus's house specifically to heal his daughter. Both Mark and Luke tell this story with an interruption—while Jairus is talking to Jesus a woman touches Jesus's robe and is healed. While Jesus speaks to her, Jairus gets the word that his daughter is dead. Still, Jesus goes to Jairus's home. Clearly, Jesus cared enough for Jairus and for his daughter to make the trip to perform this miracle. One of the most common things that Jesus did in his ministry was to heal people. It's easy to concentrate on Jesus's birth, death, and resurrection and not think much about his ministry, which often included healing. His ministry tells us a lot about the kingdom of God and that Jesus cares about both children and adults.

The Humility of Children

There are two passages in the Gospels in which Jesus speaks *about* children. Both of these passages are in all three Synoptic Gospels.[2] The first passage is about who is the greatest in the kingdom.[3]

> They came to Capernaum. When he was in the house, he asked them, "What were you arguing about on the road?" But they kept quiet because on the way they had argued about who was the greatest.
>
> Sitting down, Jesus called the Twelve and said, "If anyone wants to be first, he must be the very last, and the servant of all."
>
> He took a little child and had him stand among them. Taking him in his arms, he said to them, "Whoever welcomes one of these little children in my name welcomes me; and whoever welcomes me does not welcome me but the one who sent me."
>
> Mark 9:33–37

All teachers love "teachable moments." These are times when a student asks a question or when something happens in your class that prepares the group to listen to an important teaching. Sometimes circumstances do a better job of preparing a class for a lesson than any introduction you can muster on your own. Once on an April 15 when I was teaching seventh grade math, a student asked what a tax return was. Many of the students in the class had heard their parents or other adults use the term but really didn't know what it was. That gave me a chance to talk to my students about how the U.S. income tax system works.

The situation presented itself, they were interested, and I had a chance to teach when I knew they were listening.

When Jesus caught his disciples in this awkward discussion of greatness, he had the same type of situation and he used it as a teachable moment.

As we saw in chapter 2, Jesus's ministry and life were deeply embedded in the culture of first-century Israel. Culture is much more than just the way people dress or the language they speak. Culture also affects the way people think about things. In contrast to North Americans today, the Hebrews were, as historian Marvin Wilson says, an "energetic, robust and, at times, even turbulent people."[4] Their way of thinking about things was quite different from our twenty-first-century ways. "For them," Wilson goes on to say, "truth was not so much an idea to be contemplated as an experience to be lived, a deed to be done."[5]

To better understand Scripture, we need to learn how to think as the Hebrews thought. One example of this is when God wanted to tell Abraham about the many descendants he would have. We read about this in Genesis 15. God didn't just say, "You'll have many." When Abraham needed assurance, God took Abraham outside the tent and showed him the stars. He said, "Look up at the heavens and count the stars—if indeed you can count them." Then God said, "So shall your offspring be" (v. 5). It was very much a part of the Hebrew culture to *show and do*, rather than just to say.

Jesus taught a lot like the rabbis of his day. He was teaching first-century Hebrews, so we should expect him to teach in a way that they could best understand him.[6] Like other rabbis, he talked as he traveled, making use of objects and materials at hand to make a point. He wanted to *show and do* rather than just talk. So when Jesus caught his disciples arguing about greatness, he saw the opportunity to teach them an important lesson. Calling a child to him, he spoke about what a person's attitude needs to be to enter the kingdom of heaven. Since Jesus wanted to teach about humility, it was natural for him to use a perfect example of humility, a child.

While Jesus and those he taught were Hebrew, the Roman world had great influence on them—politically, if not in other ways. At that time in Roman culture, children were not considered full people. They had only *potential status*. Judith Gundry-Volf writes that because the ability to reason was so prized in Roman society, children were seen as "fundamentally deficient and not yet human in the full sense."[7] The Romans thought that children were *going to be* people at some point but they were not yet real people. Children were seen almost as the equivalent of slaves and were often subject to great brutality.[8] They were at the mercy of their father who had a life and death hold over them. For Romans, children were the epitome of humility.

So when Jesus's disciples thought about greatness, perhaps they were thinking about those who were great in the world at that time—the Romans. Jesus wanted to make sure that his followers saw the difference between greatness in God's kingdom and greatness in the emperor's kingdom. His point was that a child can represent greatness in the kingdom of heaven, because greatness there is measured differently than it is measured on earth. Jesus certainly treated the child differently than the Romans did. He not only took note of the child there (something that some adults today still don't do), but he took the child in his arms. It is clear that Jesus saw them as more than just "potential people."[9]

Welcoming Children

Jesus's lesson was not just about true greatness. In all three Gospels in which the story is told, Jesus speaks about "welcoming" a child.[10] He is saying that "welcoming a child" is an act of greatness.

What does it mean to welcome children? From a church perspective, welcoming children involves making them feel as though they are important and that they have a place in our fellowship. Welcoming children means that we think of their special needs as we are planning events in the life of our church. Here is an example. One of the issues in our congregation had to do with what happens in our church after morning worship. We have a very outgoing congregation, and our church architecture is such that, as we leave the sanctuary, we find ourselves in a large room from which it is nearly impossible to leave without first stopping and talking to someone.

However, by the time our worship is finished, it is about 11:45 a.m. Some of the children have been in church since 9:15 when their church school classes began. After sitting for so long, at 11:45 they have a lot of energy to get out of their system. We have a fairly small church and parents feel that their children are safe as long as they stay in the building, so letting them play out of sight is generally fine. Sometimes the children run around and aren't very careful. Once a child bumped into an older member of the congregation and the woman fell down. She wasn't badly hurt but this was clearly not an acceptable situation. We needed to address the problem before someone did get hurt.

The first thought was to ask parents to tell their children not to run at church. That made a lot of sense, so an announcement to that effect was put in our bulletin.

However, this turned out to be an ineffective solution. Even when most parents kept their children corralled, there were always a few who were still running around. Also, it was hard for parents of young children to interact with others after the worship service if they had to keep close tabs on their rambunctious children. Our church values this time for touching

43

base with each other as an opportunity to build a sense of community and to offer mutual support, but these goals could not be realized if parents had to be concerned about what their children were doing.

A few of our staff members developed a different solution, which was much more effective and is also a wonderful example of what it means to welcome children. Recognizing that children need time to play and be with their friends, they developed a program called Celebrate Children in which structured activities were provided for the children for twenty minutes every Sunday after church. These activities were fairly simple—things like Hot Wheels cars and tracks or a plastic mini-golf set—but they kept the children busy, gave them positive things to do, and allowed the children to enjoy the time after church while their parents drank coffee and visited with friends.

We asked for volunteers to supervise these activities. They also evaluated each one, so we would know if the kids enjoyed the activity and if we should use it again. In addition to providing activities for the young children, some of the activities (like the Hot Wheels track or a balloon game) attracted middle school and older students who modeled how to use these toys for the younger children.

Some of the older children really took hold of this idea. Two middle school boys came up with the idea of teaching younger children how to make paper airplanes, and that became one of the activities for a few weeks. A middle school girl thanked the leaders for coming up with this program even though it was not designed for children as old as she was. She said that she always hated the time after church because she had nothing to do while her father counted the collection money. Now she looked forward to the fun activities. The program was a great success with the children and with the parents. Not only did it solve a problem, but more important, it sent a message to the children that we see them as more than just people to be "handled" or "controlled" but people who matter.

This example might not work for your church, and perhaps it addressed a problem that you don't even have, but the point is that welcoming children and making them feel like an important part of your church community is not only a good idea, it is what Jesus commands us to do.

Let the Children Come

There is one other passage in which Jesus talks specifically about children. This passage appears in all three Synoptic Gospels.

> People were bringing little children to Jesus to have him touch them, but the disciples rebuked them. When Jesus saw this, he was indignant. He said to them, "Let the little children come to me, and do not hinder them, for the kingdom of God belongs to such as these. I tell you the truth, anyone who will not receive the kingdom of God like a little child will never enter it." And he took the children in his arms, put his hands on them and blessed them.
>
> Mark 10:13–16

Here Jesus refers specifically to children, and his comments, while brief, are specifically designed to tell his disciples, and us, something about children. In this case, the children appear to be the reason for the lesson (as opposed to the passage I discussed earlier in which Jesus called a child to him as an illustration of his point).

Apparently Jesus felt strongly about how the disciples were treating the children. This is one of only two incidents in which Jesus is shown to be angry.[11] Not only does Jesus tell his disciples not to keep the children away, but he calls the children to him, takes them in his arms, and blesses them. In Arthur Peake's commentary on this passage, we read that the verb used for "bless" is "intensive and far removed from any official benediction."[12] It seems clear that in this instance Jesus went out of his way to welcome children—something that was significant enough for three Gospel writers to include.[13]

In my research on this passage, I found that many commentators focus on what Jesus says about the kingdom rather than on what he says about children. It is remarkable how often this passage is interpreted as teaching something other than about children. For example, in its commentary on the New Testament, the Harper Bible commentary practically ignores the passage about children and focuses instead on the brief question about celibacy that precedes it.[14] Albert Barnes sees the children in this passage primarily as examples for Jesus to use to make his point. He does not discuss them as having value in themselves.[15] Roehrs and Franzmann see this passage as being an "illustration of the nature of the fellowship of the church."[16]

In this story, though, we see that Jesus goes out of his way to make sure that children are included in those who are allowed to come to him. Commentators who focus only on the other aspects of this passage are missing something important. Jesus is not calling us to have wonderful high-powered programs for children, but he is calling us to enfold our children into the life of the church. He demonstrates that they should not be shuttled off to a corner of the building or to a special program, but they should be included so that we have a truly intergenerational church. The Lord calls us to be a community, a community that involves people of all ages worshiping and working together. In this way we come to understand some of the richness and the diversity of God's people.

George Barna's research tells us that children are much more open to the message of the gospel than are either teens or adults.[17] So making our churches more child friendly is not only the right thing to do, it also makes good evangelical sense.

When I emphasize people rather than programs, I don't mean that we should not have special programs for children. A lot can be accomplished in Christian education through special programs, and it is important to have time set aside for children to be in programs that are specifically designed for them—like church school classes or special children's worship (which I'll address in chapter 7). There needs to be a balance, however. The special needs of children should be met along with their need to be part of the body of believers.

When children and young people are involved in the full life of the church, everybody wins. Children get to see that our faith is more than just something we talk about, and adults get to experience more of the body of believers. Without children present, we're missing an important part of who we are.

Our focus should be on programs that bring us together, even if individual events are designed for specific ages or gender groups. To encourage faith that becomes part of the fabric of the lives of children, to help children and young people develop a three-dimensional faith, we need to make sure that they have a place in the mainstream life of the church. If they have this place, they will be able to see that Christ is an important part of the lives of their parents, grandparents, and other adults.

4

Dwelling in the Mysteries

Principle 3: Children need to know that God is mysterious.

I grew up in a Christian tradition that puts a high value on education, thought, and reason. We know that we have a *reasonable* faith—a faith that makes sense. If we want children to have a three-dimensional faith, knowledge is essential. However, we can sometimes take this to an extreme. We think long and hard about *everything*. I'm not complaining or criticizing—that's just the way things are for the community that I grew up in and of which I am still gladly a part. Because of this, I have a natural tendency to think things through. In fact it is a source of pride that usually I can explain what I believe.

The problem is that God is too big for me to understand. I'm not suggesting that I should stop thinking about God. On the contrary, thinking about him is a really good thing. When I restrict God to merely that which I can understand, however, there is a problem, because my conception of God becomes much smaller than he really is. Fortunately, I'm aware of this tendency and I'm working on it. As I get older, I'm allowing myself to be more comfortable with the fact that I don't know some things about God and his work in the world. This is an important step for me, and it has a huge impact on the way I help children learn about God. If I introduce children to a God who is so small I can explain everything about him, I am shortchanging the children. Part of the wonder of God is that we will never fully understand him.

We need to allow ourselves and our children the awareness that there is much about God we will never know. We must give them permission to dwell in the *mystery* of God. The apostle Paul wrote, "Men ought to regard us as servants of Christ and as those entrusted with the secret things of God" (1 Cor. 4:1). Other translations use the phrase "stewards of the mysteries of God."

Faith and Doubt

God did not *intend* for me to be able to figure everything out. He knows that none of us is smart enough or insightful enough to understand the eternal. Even though I know this, I sometimes don't do a good job of passing on this sense of mystery to children. I tend to want to simplify things so that children can understand them. I also want to make sure that I don't pass on any doubts.

Since there is a lot about God that I can't explain well, often what I, and others, do is tell children something about God that is actually less than who God really is. Without intending to do so, I end up giving them a watered-down version of God, because I want to be able to explain him.

This is a mistake. Children with whom we worship need to know that we consider the things of God to be mysterious.

Actually this will nurture in them a sense of God's mystery as well. We don't need to fear that we do children a disservice by admitting there are things about God we're not so sure about. I think we give ourselves, our children, and even God less credit than we should if we think our openness will inhibit their faith. Anne Lamott addresses the notion of faith and doubt in her book *Plan B: Further Thoughts on Faith*. She writes,

> I have a lot of faith. But I am also afraid a lot, and have no real certainty about anything. I remembered something Father Tom had told me—*that the opposite of faith is not doubt, but certainty. Certainty is missing the point entirely.* Faith includes noticing the mess, the emptiness and discomfort, and letting it be there until some light returns.[1]

Whether you want to argue with Lamott's assertion that the opposite of faith is certainty or not, the point is still the same, doubt is part of faith. God knows this and you and I know it. The question is not will there be doubt; the question is how will we deal with it?

Understanding Development

I have found James Fowler's theory of faith development helpful in this regard.[2] In his landmark book, *Stages of Faith*, Fowler suggests that there are different stages of faith that people experience as they age and grow.[3] Before we look at Fowler's stages, we need to think briefly about developmental theories in general. Developmental theories, no matter what aspect of development they consider, share some general principles:[4]

1. *People develop at different rates.* One of the issues in development is that everyone does not change at the same time. This makes sense if you think of physical growth.

Laura and I have twins, a boy and a girl, who had different growth patterns. Our daughter, Meredith, grew very quickly and was one of the tallest girls in her class when she was in elementary and middle school. Her twin brother, Bryan, grew later, not really taking off until his first two years of high school. After being shorter than his sister for the first fifteen years of their lives, he caught up quickly and is now taller than she is, something he points out often. They both grew; it is just that the rates of growth were different.

Other types of physical development can also occur at different rates for different people. Some children begin to talk before others do. Some walk early and others walk late. Mental and emotional development occurs at different rates as well.

2. *Development is orderly.* Children learn to roll over before they crawl. They crawl before they walk. We expect accomplishments like these to happen in a particular order. This is not only true for physical development, it is also true for emotional and cognitive skills. For example, babies are not as good as toddlers at remembering things that they cannot see. That's one reason babies are surprised and entertained by peek-a-boo. Not too many teenagers would get a kick out of that game. After children learn to hold things in their memory longer, they are able to learn to do other more challenging mental tasks. The point is that we can generally depend on some things happening before other things as children develop.

3. *Development takes place gradually.* Changes don't happen overnight. While we can talk about people being in this or that stage of development, it is clear that these things take time. One example of this is when a boy's

voice changes. Laura and I remember hearing Bryan, as a Little League catcher, calling out instructions to the team. We laughed because he was trying to be a leader and get the team excited but did it with a high-pitched young boy's voice. Now that he's almost twenty, his voice sounds a lot like mine, so people mistake him for me, not his mother, on the phone. But as his voice was changing, it sometimes cracked when he spoke or sang. This was evidence that a change was in process. It's this way with all types of development; change is gradual.

Because some physical changes are pretty easy for us to see but others are not so obvious, we may think that there are only two stages of development—a child stage and an adult stage. Actually there are often many more stages. It is also easy to think of development as something that happens just to children because our physical development is mostly in place by the time we reach adulthood. Faith development, though, according to James Fowler, often continues on through the adult years.[5]

Fowler's Faith Development Stages

Here are the six faith development stages that Fowler identifies:

Stage 1—Intuitive-Projective Faith (ages 2–6). This stage is primarily a reflection of parental faith and is a stage filled with fantasy, imagination, and powerful images.

Stage 2—Mythic-Literal Faith (ages 6–12). In this stage the circle of influence widens to include others besides parents. Children (and some adults) in this stage believe strongly in what they have been told. Their faith is straightforward and includes few gray areas.

Stage 3—Synthetic-Conventional Faith (ages 12–?). The importance of belonging to a group typifies this stage when it takes place in adolescence. In adults it shows itself to be a faith that has a strong sense of being part of a community of believers. Belonging to the group and agreeing with what the group believes is important at this stage.

Stage 4—Individuative-Reflective Faith (ages 18–?). In this stage people take personal responsibility for their own faith. This often shows itself as a time of questioning and exploring.

Stage 5—Conjunctive Faith (ages 30–?). In this stage people are able to see that many of the faith practices that they doubted or threw off in their time of questioning are much richer and more valuable than they were able to see at a younger age. This is the stage in which people own their faith.

Stage 6—Universalizing Faith (ages ??). Faith becomes more than just a set of beliefs but is a total commitment. This occurs in few members of the population.

As you can see in Fowler's list of stages, the third stage of faith (synthetic-conventional) is a period of intense loyalty. People in this stage tend to see many things in terms of the group or in terms of some external source of authority. In all of the first three stages, authority is located outside of the individual. In other words, people in these stages are ultimately responsible to someone else. Some other person or people—parents, pastor, older sibling—are really in charge of the big decisions in their life.

Fowler's fourth stage (which he called individuative-reflective faith) isn't part of what children experience, but when we understand this stage, it can have a profound impact on how we minister to children. People reach this stage, if it is reached at all, in early adulthood,[6] when they begin to take authority for their own actions. It has been dubbed "the critic"[7] and can be frightening for parents and those who minister to young adults.

An example of taking personal responsibility occurred when my middle daughter, Meredith, was in the first months of her freshman year in college. She wasn't feeling well and wanted to know whether she should go to class. When Meredith was younger, there was no question that if she didn't feel well, she would talk to Laura or me about it, and we would determine if she was allowed to stay home from school. The decision was ours to make, and she expected that we would do so. When children get older, such a decision is no longer the parents' responsibility but that of the child. Meredith knew (more or less) that it was her decision to make but she wanted help in making it, so we had a long conversation about it before she finally decided.

This is similar to how young adults think about their faith. There is a point in our lives, at least for most of us, when we take personal responsibility for our beliefs. For the first time, we ask ourselves what we truly believe. Before this, our faith was mostly unquestioned. From the perspective of young believers, they wouldn't think about the reality of their faith any more than they would think about wanting to breathe. In *Reviving Ophelia* Mary Pipher writes that at thirteen she was a "loyal Methodist," but as she got older, she began reading things that challenged her faith and she debated with her pastor and her friends about the existence of God.[8] Pipher articulated what a number of young people go through. In her case she seems to have questioned her faith beyond the point of being able to accept it. As young adults begin to ask these questions, people in positions of authority—parents, pastors, teachers, and others—

can be uncomfortable with the idea of exploring the validity of these central issues of faith.

What about Middle School and High School?

Often the period of searching faith happens when people reach college age. Does that mean that middle and high school students aren't choosing their own faith? The theories indicate (and recent research supports) that teenagers generally arrive at a stage where they do indeed choose their faith—but their choices are limited to basically the one faith that they grew up with. So older children continue to follow the faith of their parents, but they are beginning to take ownership of that faith.

Whether or not this makes people uncomfortable, it seems clear that when young people accept the responsibility for their faith, questions will arise. Both James Fowler and John Westerhoff include a period of "searching faith" in their writing about faith development.[9] At this point many people take a step back from the faith in which they were raised. This is not to say that everyone throws off their beliefs, but there is a time in our lives when we consider whether our faith community, the one we grew up in, perhaps, or the one in which we are currently involved, teaches the truth. It is a natural part of development. This fact has important things to say to us about ministry to children and about dealing with the mystery of God.

Incomplete Messages

Given what we know about faith development, it does not seem wise to teach children about a faith that has no room for mystery. God *is* mysterious. The Bible *is* a book full of wonder. As I study the stories of the Old Testament, for example, I find myself wondering why some of the stories are even included. It is difficult for me to understand why, for example, God used Samson, a man who seems to be little more than an arrogant adulterer, to be the deliverer of Israel. Why did God allow Jacob to be tricked into marrying Leah when it would lead to such misery for her? Why did Solomon, who was wise in so many ways, not see what was happening to him with all his marriages to foreign women? The list goes on and on. Prominent Bible characters, whom we often hold up as models for how we should live, still are shown to have flaws that would make most of us hide our heads in shame.

It's not just the Old Testament that is mysterious. Jesus's actions and sayings are sometimes hard to figure out. His parables, for example, are often filled with ideas and images that make us wonder. He picked only twelve people to be his special close disciples, and yet one of those people betrayed him. How is that possible? Didn't he know what he was doing when he picked Judas? Or perhaps he did know what he was doing. It's a puzzle. These things are deep mysteries.

The Bible isn't just a novel with curious things in it. This is the book that gives us the complete text of what God wants us to know about him and his work with his people. The parts that are mysterious are there for a reason. Hiding these mysterious aspects of God from children gives them an incomplete picture of who he is. It is not only *acceptable* for children to see that God is mysterious but it is *essential.* This sense of mystery does not need to lead to puzzlement; it can also foster a healthy sense of wonder and awe at God's greatness.

Allowing children to meet only an explainable God does them a great disservice when they reach the point of asking questions. In Brian McLaren's book *The Story We Find Ourselves In*, we read an account of Kerry, a young woman who was raised in a pastor's family and was targeted by an overzealous youth pastor, Steve, to adopt a very strict view of who God is and of how the world was put together.[10] She had a natural tendency to question and explore, but Steve would tell her: "You can't have it both ways. It's either God's wisdom or man's. It's either God's authoritative Word or man's autonomous word." Kerry believed Steve's views until she came across some information that didn't seem to fit into the particular view of God that he had taught her. McLaren writes, "In an instant, her faith seemed to disappear, to evaporate, and she was left with nothing."[11]

Giving children like Kerry a thin understanding of God can be a recipe for a broken faith later on. Letting children see that we don't have it all figured out gives them permission to live with questions at the same time that they hold on to what they do know—that God loves them and that he is holding them in his hand. This allows their faith to grow so that it doesn't buckle with the first questions. A thin understanding of God is not necessarily wrong, but it is incomplete. There is much more to God than the things we can understand fully.

Keeping the Message Complex

Incomplete messages about the nature of God don't come just from parents and teachers. Often Christian media oversimplify things, especially media aimed at children. When our children were younger, Laura and I would play Christian tapes for children when we traveled in the car. One tape was particularly troubling. On this tape a young boy told a story about losing his softball. According to the boy in the story, he closed his eyes and prayed that God would help him find his ball. He opened his eyes and looked down and . . . there it was!

If only life were that simple! Things would be much easier if we could solve all our problems with a simple heartfelt prayer. But our lives include disappointments, even if we are people of prayer. We have all prayed about things that haven't worked out the way we'd hoped. We pray for people who continue to deny God's place in their lives. Friends and relatives get sick and die despite fervent prayers. If we talk about a God who automatically helps children find lost baseballs, how do we face a child who is dealing with much more serious issues? What do we tell a child whose parents are divorced or who has been abused? What do we say to a child whose parent has died?

Imagine the kinds of thoughts that go through the mind of a child who listens over and over to messages like the one about the softball. *If God cares enough to find a softball for the little boy whose heart was really turned toward God, then is it my fault that my friend got sick? Is it my fault that my parents got divorced? Didn't I pray hard enough? Did I not believe enough?*

These are some of the things that even adults do not understand. Understanding exactly what happens in prayer is tricky. Turning the results of prayer into a test of personal piety is bad for any of us, especially children, who have limited understanding, and it is not theologically sound. I'm sure the creators of the tape in question never meant to imply that answers to prayer are based on how well you are doing on any piety scale, but that's the message that comes through. By simplifying what it means to be a Christian, we replace a deep understanding of faith with a very thin version. Life is complex and so is God.

We see the complexities in the lives of people we know as well as those in biblical stories. Jacob, for example, is a *very* complex person. He lied to his father about who he was. His brother Esau was so angry at him that Jacob had to leave his home. He cheated his Uncle Laban and tried to manipulate the flocks that he was charged with watching so that his share would be greater than his uncle's. He married two sisters and treated his children differently, depending on who their mother was. He believed that a wild animal had killed his son Joseph, whom he loved, when in fact Joseph's brothers had sold him into slavery.

Jacob isn't the only example of a life filled with struggles and sorrow in the Bible. There are many in the Bible. There are many in Jacob's family! A good read through the Bible makes it clear that a life of faith isn't easy. It isn't all about instant answers to prayer and happy-clappy worship times. Sometimes we struggle with the way things are and why God has allowed them to happen. Sometimes we sin and make the wrong choices. Often we wish that our faith came with an "easy button," but it doesn't.

It is, of course, one thing to live with the mystery of why God does some things and quite another to live with questions about whether God exists or if he cares about us. It can be a challenge, but a worthwhile one, to ask how God might be working through or in spite of the kinds of situations we read about in the Old Testament. We saw earlier that Mary Pipher's Methodist faith at age thirteen couldn't survive the questions that arose when she was older. We do not want to give children a *weak* faith; we want to give them a *rich* faith, a faith that acknowledges that there is much about God and the way he works that we do not know.

That's one of the real strengths of Old Testament stories in working with children. The people in these stories don't always act the way they should. They don't always do what God wants them to do. They do, however, know that God exists. David never doubts God's place in his life, even when he sins with Bathsheba. Joseph's brothers still knew God, even when they placed Joseph in the pit and sold him into slavery. Samson knew God's strength, though he took for himself the credit for his own feats of strength. These people didn't act the way they should—and they often paid the price for it—but the place of God in their lives was clear. The people in these stories knew that God is the God of the universe and that he cared about them as a people and as individuals. If we live with these stories as part of the ebb and flow of our lives, we can see that God is working in our lives in the same way that he worked in the lives of Joseph, David, and Samson. By letting children see, in age-appropriate ways, that the heroes of the Bible are all real people just like us, we give them a clearer idea that God is a God who works in the lives of his people.

Children have a limited ability to understand difficult things—we adults do too! When we give children only the stories of God miraculously answering prayers, we give them a false image of God as someone who sometimes seems to care and sometimes does not. This is a poor way to build faith. The truth is that we just don't know why God allows some bad things to happen and keeps other bad things from happening. It is good to let children know that there are things about God, like this, that we don't know. It is also good for us and, when age appropriate, our children to read the wealth of wonderful material written by people who have struggled with these mysteries and have good things to say about their struggles.

Complex doesn't have to mean complicated. We can let children in on the fact that God is mysterious without making his story complicated, and we need to simplify the story without letting it be simplistic. Telling Bible stories about people like Joseph, people who led lives that sometimes seem a lot like ours, is an effective and authentic way to help children come to terms with the mysteries of God.

If we want our children to have a three-dimensional faith, a faith that lives within them in a way that seems real and impacts all aspects of their life, we must teach them in ways that let them see how much bigger God is than we can understand. The community of faith has to gather around children when they become teenagers and start to ask questions about whether the faith they've grown up in is really *their* faith. The community has to be willing to walk alongside these teens when they ask questions and not scold them or tell them that they must not think about such things. But before they become teenagers, we have to give children the knowledge that their older brothers and sisters in Christ are not troubled by questions. Questions are one way we have of thinking about who God is and his place in our lives. We must let them know that we have questions too, but we know God is bigger than our questions, even when we don't know the answers.

5

The Power of Story

Principle 4: Bible stories are the key to helping children know a God who is mysterious and who knows them for who they are.

My father-in-law told the same stories for years. Many of them were about his time in the army during World War II, when he met his future wife while he was serving in Denver. As he got older, he told these stories with more frequency. He used the same words and phrases each time. "I was on my way out of church and a pretty sixteen-year-old girl tripped me. And I fell for her." Every one of his children and grandchildren can recite the whole story, practically word for word.

My parents had stories too that I learned as I grew up. I remember clearly their story about having to pay for the natural gas for their apartment by putting a quarter into a meter. They kept a quarter on top of the meter so that when they ran out, they would have the coin handy. Sometimes they had to borrow that quarter to use for other needs, hoping they would be able to replace it before the gas ran out!

Knowing these stories is part of being a member of our family. They help us understand who we are. They help us understand our parents, our grandparents, and each other. There are stories from Laura's family that I have heard so many times that they feel like my story.

Families are like that. No one studies to be a member of a family. We live our lives surrounded by our parents and siblings, our aunts, uncles, and cousins. Living in community we learn what we need to know about how our family works. The stories that we share are simply part of who we are.

Moralizing Stories

Our culture has a long history of telling stories. Much of the time the purpose for the story is the specific moral lesson at the end. Fables are often told with "and the moral of the story is . . ." as the closing line. Stories are an incredibly powerful way of communicating ideas. We hear a story and we remember it. Consequently we often remember the attached moral as well. Sometimes we remember the moral, which in turn, triggers a memory of the story. For example, if you hear, "Slow and steady wins the race," you might quickly think of the story of the tortoise and the hare. We often link story and moral so tightly that we look for a lesson at the end of each fablelike story, whether it is there or not. For those who want to teach a moral lesson, story is an obvious and effective way. This is the reason so many of our culture's stories contain morals— because it is an effective way of communicating.

Jesus knew this, of course, and used stories, which are called parables, to help us understand God's kingdom. However, not all stories are parables or fables. Not every story is told with

64

the purpose of teaching a particular lesson. The stories that my father-in-law told about his time in the army, for example, were not told to teach his grandchildren anything other than a little bit about who he was and what his life was like. He didn't tell these stories to show what a good guy he was—in fact some of the stories are about his sneaking off the army base (although he often did this to go to church on Sunday mornings). He told these stories *because they happened.* This is true of many of the stories that we hear from friends, relatives, and others. The stories don't always have a point. People tell the stories because they happened.

Through the stories we read in the Bible, we learn about who God is in relationship to his people and about what it means to live as his children. We also learn how his people have fallen short of what God wants them to be. The primary purpose for stories in the Bible is to convey the knowledge of God and of our relationship to him. A lot of the stories are not included so that we can extract a moral lesson. In fact trying to find such a lesson can rob a story of its very character *as a story*, is unfair to the text itself, and may turn God into little more than a sort of cosmic policeman who is more concerned with our allegiance to a set of rules than with his relationship to us. There are many things that we can learn from a story without turning it into a mere moral tale. Let's look at an example of a story from the Bible that is told because it happened—the story of the Israelites' battle with the Amalekites in Exodus 17:8–13:

> The Amalekites came and attacked the Israelites at Rephidim. Moses said to Joshua, "Choose some of our men and go out to fight the Amalekites. Tomorrow I will stand on top of the hill with the staff of God in my hands."
>
> So Joshua fought the Amalekites as Moses had ordered, and Moses, Aaron and Hur went to the top of the hill. As long

as Moses held up his hands, the Israelites were winning, but whenever he lowered his hands, the Amalekites were winning. When Moses' hands grew tired, they took a stone and put it under him and he sat on it. Aaron and Hur held his hands up—one on one side, one on the other—so that his hands remained steady till sunset. So Joshua overcame the Amalekite army with the sword.

This brief story tells how God delivered his people from their enemies. If we were intent on deriving a moral from this story, it would be something like "it is good to have others to lean on," or perhaps we could say, "So, boys and girls, look at how important it is that we have Christian friends who can help us like Moses's friends helped him." If we said that, though, we would be overlooking a lot of the story. It is true that Moses had his two friends help him, but this story is more than that. (Notice, I didn't write that the story is *about* more than that—the story *is* more than that.) In this story God used Moses's arms and his friends' support to show his power to the people. It was obvious to all the people that it wasn't primarily their military might that was winning the battle. We also see that Joshua, who later became the leader of Israel, was present and involved in this story. I wonder what Joshua learned that day. Did he learn something about how God can change the outcome of a battle? Did this prepare him for his later life?[1] Moses somehow knew to raise his hands to affect the way the battle was going. How did he know that? Did God tell him to do it?

As we read or hear this story, we realize the important role that Aaron and Hur played. We see how they helped their friend and brother at a time when his strength wasn't enough. It really *is* good to have friends to lean on. And it really is important to have good friends who love the Lord and share our faith and can hold us up when our strength isn't sufficient.

If children are told that this story is all about having someone to lean on, however, they are not invited to think about what happened or ponder what God may be teaching them. When we attach a particular moral to the end of a story, children think we are telling them what the story *really* means, and as a consequence, the other wonderful things in the story are eliminated from consideration. The children recite the lesson back whenever they hear the story, and this recitation keeps them from thinking deeply about it.

We need to remember that a story such as this is not intended as a lesson plan; it's history. We need to learn to be comfortable with the idea that the stories in the Bible are not treatises on moral values—they are the stories of God's people. Understanding the stories in the Bible *as story* is essential to understanding God's word to us and, consequently, an important part of ministry to children.

Using Story to Communicate Ideas

God chose to tell us about himself through story. Much of the Bible, certainly the historical part of the Old Testament and the Gospels, is made up of stories. Through the stories of what God did and what his people did, God introduces himself to us. To better understand the Bible, we need to remember that the people who wrote it and who first read the Bible had a different mind-set than we do. The world in which the human writers of the Bible lived was quite different from the world you and I live in. This is the reason we are sometimes encouraged to "think Hebrew" to help us understand the Bible in the way that the first readers did.

Even though the Bible is set in a particular time and place, the stories and writings contained in it are true and remain relevant today.[2] They are not just stories that are *placed* in a particular setting, like a historical novel, perhaps. These stories were first *told and written* in this particular setting.[3] The setting isn't just tangential to the story. Understanding the setting is often crucial to understanding the story.

During the period of time that the Bible was written, people often used stories to tell about something that was complex. In some ways we still do that. Recently I was at the wedding of my nephew Tim. When his best man got up to speak at the wedding reception, he said he was going to tell a story about Tim that would help us all understand him better. Like many college students, Tim and his roommates had a cheap television that would sometimes get fuzzy because of poor reception. At these times someone would have to get up and hit the set on the side to get it to work well again. Tim didn't like getting up to fix the set, so one day he got two pencils and duct-taped them to the ceiling, one over the TV set and one over the couch. He took string and tied one end to a shoe and he strung the other end over the two pencils, dropping the end down by the couch on which they sat to watch TV. So when the TV set got fuzzy, he no longer had to get up to fix it; he could just pull on the string and drop the shoe on top of the TV.

Stories like this helped all of us at the wedding understand Tim a bit better. The difference between our culture and the ancient Hebrew culture is that Tim's best man felt the need to introduce the story by telling us that he had a story that would help us understand Tim better. In Old Testament times they would just have told the story. Since using story to communicate information was such a part of the Hebrew culture, it makes sense that God would use story to tell us about himself. Even today we see that story is an inherently powerful way to communicate rich and complex ideas. In addition to communicating ideas, stories bring an aesthetic dimension that a lecture doesn't. Stories can carry emotion and beauty and something intangible that other ways of communicating ideas do not convey.

Using Story with Children

The literature about ministry to children is rich with references to the importance of story. Catherine Stonehouse writes, "stories are at the heart of faith development for children."[4] Our understanding of development supports Stonehouse's assertion. Children have a view of their faith that is often made up of unarticulated images, either visual or narrative. It is in the stories that the core of children's faith is kept.

Harvard psychologist Robert Coles found that children relate the experiences of biblical characters to the events of their own lives.[5] The power of story goes beyond age and race. It can help bring together people from different times and places because the people who live in these stories are just like you and me. Through the words of a masterful storyteller, we cross the Jordan River with the Israelites, we climb the tree with Zacchaeus, and we stand at the foot of the cross with Jesus's disciples.

Jerome Berryman stresses the importance of the oral tradition of storytelling.[6] Many of us love to listen to someone tell a captivating story. Most of the time these stories are not in formal storytelling settings. They happen when we get together and talk with friends or family. And when someone tells a story in a more formal setting, we often perk up and listen. I know that I usually pay attention to sermons that include stories. Not only do I pay attention better, I remember it longer.

I have a friend who is an outstanding preacher, but even when he preaches, I sometimes find my attention fading in and out. However, when he tells stories, especially good ones, I tune in and don't forget. I well remember a story he told of his young son who left the church nursery to go to the bathroom while his father was preaching. He came out of the bathroom with his pants down around his ankles and, hearing his father's voice, marched himself up to the pulpit to get his father's help. When Dad bent down to help his son, he said, "What do you need?" and his son replied, "My shoe is untied." The point my friend was making in his sermon was that when we approach God, we don't always know what we need most. Without the story about his son, I might not have heard his point and I'm pretty sure I wouldn't remember it now. A story grabs our attention in ways that other forms of speech cannot.[7]

Jerome Berryman also writes about the role that silence plays in the spiritual life of children.[8] He urges us not to rush our stories but to give children time and space to think and to live in the story. This is an important point, I think. If we rush through stories, we can inadvertently suggest to children that we need to get through the story quickly so that we can get to "the lesson." But stories should be more meaningful than just an introduction to a lesson. We want children to be able to put themselves into the story. As we help children see the breadth and depth of the stories of God, the stories begin to merge and become a "story of the stories." The power of this group of stories is even greater than the sum of its parts, as the ideas of who God is and who we are begin to emerge more clearly through the telling and retelling of these stories. It is in this way that we meet God.

Effective Storytelling

Some people are more effective storytellers than others, but with thought and practice, even a novice can become a good storyteller. The most important thing you can do in telling stories is to be thoughtful about it. Think through the things you want to accomplish with your story. Prepare ahead of time by reading the story through a couple of times. If possible, do some background reading. Learning a bit about the connections between stories and the culture in which they took place can add a lot to your understanding, and that will come out in the way you tell the story. In general, pay attention to storytelling mechanics, think about the setting, edit your story, place each story in its larger context, and get to know the characters.

Storytelling Mechanics

There are some basic public speaking and storytelling mechanics that you should think about the first few times you tell stories. As you practice, they will become more natural and you won't have to worry about them so much.

Eye contact: If you keep good eye contact with your listeners, they will feel that you are telling them a story rather than giving a speech. You want your listeners to pay attention, so you have to engage them by looking at them and not your notes. This means you will have to know your story really well.

Your voice: Think about how fast you speak and the volume of your voice. I tend to talk fast, and I have had to train myself to slow down. Speaking slowly and pausing occasionally helps your listeners take in and visualize what you are saying. You may think you are going too slowly, but it will not seem that way to the listeners, who are trying to process what you are telling them. There are storytellers, however, who can get so ponderous that their listeners practically fall asleep waiting for something to happen in the story. Listen to a tape, or better yet, watch a video of your storytelling. This will put you in the place of your listeners and you will see ways to improve. Pay attention to your listeners as you are telling a story; if they seem to lose interest, it may be that the pace of your storytelling is too fast or too slow.

Setting

As you think about your story, paint a picture in your mind of how things look. Then you can help your listeners see it too. This is where doing research can be very helpful. Finding out how people lived during the time that your story happened will let you imagine things more realistically. As you are telling the story, if you imagine that the Sea of Galilee is on your left, motion to it when you talk about it as if you were standing on the shore. By seeing the scene in your mind, you can build a real place for your listeners. Sometimes when I'm telling a Bible story to my college class, I ask them afterward where something was located, and they always know. Because I had imagined it clearly in a certain spot in the room and referred to it as I told the story, before long they could see it there too.

Don't spend too much time describing the setting. You want to get to the action of your story. Some details are important, of course, but going overboard doesn't accomplish much. Just because you can "see it" doesn't mean you have to describe all the details. But if you see the scene in your mind, there's a better chance that your listeners will too.

The Importance of Editing

Sometimes, from a storyteller's perspective, there just isn't enough detail in the stories in the Bible. We'd love to know more, for example, about Rahab. The only things we know about her are that she was a prostitute who hid the spies in Jericho. Later it turns out that she is one of the ancestors of Jesus. It sure would be interesting to know more about her.

How did her induction into the Hebrew culture go? Was she readily accepted or was it hard on her? Why were the spies at her house anyway? There really isn't enough information in the story to help a storyteller have a fully developed character.

On the other hand, many Bible stories contain a lot of information or interrelated ideas that can cause the stories to be pretty long and involved. Many of these are told in several chapters in the Bible. There is just too much information for you to include in the story. If you tell it all, it is a recipe for sleepy listeners. As you tell a story, think about the part of the story where you really want your children to focus. Then choose the pieces of the backstory that will focus their attention to your main point. You can edit out the other parts, leaving the core of the story.

In my work as a college professor, I work with students who are preparing to be teachers. In my Religious Education class, I hear them each tell Bible stories every semester. Sometimes of course the results are less than inspiring, but often, as my students tell familiar stories, they focus my attention on new aspects of the story. The words they use or their facial expressions as they tell some aspect of what happened long ago cause me to think about the story in a new way. I often find myself asking new questions about why God placed a particular story in the Bible or why a character acted the way he or she did.

Editing Bible stories has its dangers of course. Since we believe that the Bible is the inspired Word of God, we don't want to change it or delete parts. But telling a Bible story is different from reading the Bible. Telling a story gives us the opportunity to interpret and elaborate on certain parts of the story while skipping other parts entirely. When we do this with a story from God's Word, we need to be especially careful to capture the spirit of what the Bible says in the text. That's where prayer and study are especially helpful. We want our storytelling to represent accurately what God is telling us in a particular story.

A well-told short story will make more of an impression than one that goes on and on. So, for example, if you're telling young children the story of Joseph and his brothers, you may not even need to mention Potiphar's wife. On the other hand, if you have the luxury of having a number of storytelling sessions with the same children, you can develop characters and situations from one telling to the next. There is much more to deciding what to include in your story than simply reading the text.

The Story's Context

Even though we don't want to make our stories unnecessarily long, it can be very helpful for children, especially older children, if the stories can be placed in a larger biblical context. So, for example, in telling the story of Deborah in Judges 4 or any of the other judges, you might open your story like this:

"God had brought his people from Israel to the Promised Land. He brought them on dry land through the Jordan River and instructed them to clear the land that they found on the other side and claim it. And they did that—sort of. You see, God's people kept forgetting about God and they turned away from him until one of their neighbors made life very difficult for them. The kings of the nearby people would enslave the Israelites and make them work for them instead of for themselves or for God. The people were miserable and would finally remember God and turn to him. Each time, God heard their cry and sent a deliverer. We sometimes call these deliverers the judges. After God saved his people, they soon forgot about him again and another king from the region took over their land and made them very unhappy. This happened over and over again in the book of Judges. In today's story the people of God once again turned away from God, and God allowed them to fall into the hands of Jabin, a king of Canaan."

With an introduction like this, the story is placed in the context of the book of Judges and of the larger Old Testament story. Without this sort of context, the story just becomes another disconnected story from the Bible. If we want our students to grow into an understanding that these stories become part of the larger biblical narrative and part of the salvation story, we have to give them a map for how the pieces fit together. This is a good way to start.

The Story's Characters

The people from the stories in the Bible really existed. They are a lot like the people we meet every day. This may seem obvious, but when I was a boy, it never occurred to me that the people in the stories I heard were a lot like me. Bible characters seemed to say and do things quite unlike things that the people I knew said and did. I never made animal sacrifices, as did many of the people in the Old Testament. I never lay on my side for days at a time just to make a point, as Ezekiel did. This is partly because of cultural differences (although in reality, I don't think many people in Ezekiel's time did it either). The people in these stories simply didn't live the way I lived. They didn't drive cars or go to school. They wore different clothes and some of them seemed to be thinking about God all the time. There were a lot of things that made them unlike me.

I came to realize, however, that there were things we had in common. Mostly I understood that the people in these stories had feelings similar to ours today. We may never fight against a giant but we know what it's like to be afraid when we have something big staring us in the face. We may never be healed of leprosy but we know what it means to be grateful. We may not hear God's voice out loud, but there are times in my life when God has spoken to me through friends, family, and circumstances. There are some basic things that the characters in the Bible experienced that all of us can relate to. As storytellers we need to make sure these things are in our stories as we tell them. Simply put, as we tell Bible stories, we need to make sure that we have *real people* in them.

As I mentioned earlier, this can be tricky because the facts included in the stories in the Bible tend to be sparse and we get only those details that were important to the writer. Consequently we know little, for example, about Ehud except that he was left-handed. Let's look at this story and see how we can make the character more three-dimensional.

In Judges 3:12–15 we read:

> Once again the Israelites did evil in the eyes of the LORD, and because they did this evil the LORD gave Eglon king of Moab power over Israel. Getting the Ammonites and Amalekites to join him, Eglon came and attacked Israel, and they took possession of the City of Palms. The Israelites were subject to Eglon king of Moab for eighteen years.
>
> Again the Israelites cried out to the LORD, and he gave them a deliverer—Ehud, a left-handed man, the son of Gera the Benjamite.

We are told nothing of how Ehud was selected or how he felt about being part of this plot. When we're telling this story we want to be very careful not to just make things up to fill in the gaps, but we can think out loud as we tell the story. Consider the following as a way of introducing the character of Ehud.

"The people of Israel once again didn't listen to God or live the way he wanted them to live. God allowed the Moabites and their king Eglon to attack Israel and take them captive. They had to work hard for King Eglon and give him a lot of their animals and crops. They were miserable and, as they had before, they cried out to God for help, and God gave them a deliverer. His name was Ehud.

"I wonder how Ehud knew that God had this special job for him to do. I wonder if maybe Ehud heard God's voice. Maybe God told Ehud to do this by having his friends or his family tell him that they thought it would be a good idea if he gathered some of the other men in Israel and did something about this wicked King Eglon. Maybe Ehud just had a feeling inside of him that he needed to do something, and this feeling grew and grew until he acted on it. The Bible doesn't tell us how Ehud knew that he should deliver Israel, but it does tell us that God sent Ehud to do this job.

"We don't know much about Ehud. We don't know if he was tall or short. We don't know if he was a soldier or if he was a farmer. In fact one of the few things that we know is that he was left-handed! That seems like a pretty strange thing to know about him but it turns out that it's pretty important in our story."

You can see in this example that we haven't added to the story at all. It should be pretty clear to the listeners where the information from the Bible stops and my imagination begins. By spending time thinking out loud with the listeners, I have allowed them to see that Ehud is someone who is a lot like us. Few of us have heard God's voice, but many of us have had a sense growing inside us that there is something we just need to do. We have all been encouraged at one time or another by friends or family to strike out and try something new. These are things that we all feel and so did Ehud—if not in this instance then certainly in others. I've never met a political assassin and I think it's pretty unlikely that I will, but when I think about what is going on inside Ehud's head, he becomes a lot more like me. If we tell the story without thinking about Ehud *as a person,* he appears to be unlike anyone we know. By making him three-dimensional, we see that he is more like someone we might meet today. As the people in the Bible become more real to us, the stories become more real, and we recognize more fully that God cares about people just like us.

Storytelling is a powerful and effective way to help children—and adults too—build a three-dimensional faith. It helps them see that God knows about us. He knows all of our weaknesses but he desires to have a relationship with us despite our failures. Giving children access to Bible stories that have real people in them is another way to help them see that their faith is real, part of the fabric of their lives. It allows them to realize that a relationship with God is more than just head knowledge and also more than just emotions. If they see that real people in the Bible have a relationship with God that affects every part of their lives, it makes sense that God can be in every part of our lives too.

6

Obedience and Faith

Principle 5: Faith and moral development are both important but they are not the same thing.

My wife and I both taught in a small Christian school for a number of years early in our teaching careers. While she was teaching third grade, the school decided to have a fundraiser run-a-thon. Students were asked to gather pledges related to how far they would run around the school track. On the fundraising form, the students were asked to estimate how far they could run. A few of the boys, flush with the excitement of the event and the opportunity to prove their ability as runners, wrote down a number of laps that far exceeded what any adult knew they were capable of running. In an effort to get them to write down a more reasonable number, my wife tried to convince them that their estimate was too high. They insisted that they could, indeed, run that far—perhaps even farther. Finally, to get them to write down something more realistic, my wife pointed out that if they wrote down a number that was too high, people wouldn't pledge as much per lap thinking that they would have to pay more. They'd raise more money, she said, if they wrote a more reasonable number.

The unfortunate result of this line of reasoning was that some of the third graders decided that the best way to raise money, therefore, was to deliberately underestimate how far they could run, trying to dupe unsuspecting donors into giving more money. Eventually the staff was able to encourage the students to make accurate estimates, but this episode gives us some insight into the moral development of children.

Moral Development

Lawrence Kohlberg developed a theory of moral development that is much like other developmental theories.[1] People pass through the stages in an orderly way, although the rate varies. Kohlberg said that until about ages seven or eight,[2] the source of authority in moral choices is *self-interest*. This is clearly seen in the run-a-thon story. It was the boys' self interest that had them put a high number down for their estimates. They wanted to prove to themselves and anyone else who looked at their sheet that they could run very far. It wasn't until their self-interest was addressed in a different way that they were willing to make a change in their estimates.

The following is a summary of Kohlberg's stages of moral development:

Preconventional Morality
> *Stage 1—avoiding punishment.* People make moral judgments on the basis of the physical consequences of their actions.

Stage 2—reciprocity. People make moral judgments on the basis of satisfying their own needs and wants.

Conventional Morality

Stage 3—good boy / nice girl. People make moral judgments on the basis of wanting others to think they're good people.

Stage 4—law and order. People make moral judgments on the basis of external authority. Society works best when people obey the mutually agreed on rules.

Postconventional Morality

Stage 5—social contract and individual rights. People make moral judgments based not so much on laws as on the principles behind them.

Stage 6—universal ethical principles. People make moral judgments based on self-chosen ethical principles, such as human rights and the dignity of all people.

Kohlberg's work helps us understand that self-interest drives children to make certain choices. In many cases this self-interest concerns getting caught doing something and being punished for it. I remember watching one of my young daughters reach for the television on switch that she knew she wasn't supposed to touch. She'd reach out for it and before she'd actually touch it, she'd look at my wife or at me to see if she would be punished for doing this forbidden thing. Often she would follow through with her outlawed behavior, so apparently the joy she got from turning on the television and running away from us outweighed the discomfort she experienced from the time-out that was her punishment. Most parents can tell such stories. It seems pretty clear that, at least much of the time, children are driven primarily by self-interest.

As we'll see in the next chapter, when Jean Piaget wrote about cognitive development, he suggested that children at this age do not have the mental ability to take someone else's perspective.[3] They have no choice; they just can't do it. Faulting children for this is like faulting them for not being six feet tall. Without the ability to take on someone else's perspective, it is very difficult to make choices based on anything other than self-interest.[4]

As children grow and reach the second level of moral development, conventional morality (about the time they reach adolescence), they are better able to see that there are external standards. Children begin to explore these standards as they are expressed in laws, rules, and mores. At first, these standards are what children observe around them. As they grow, they begin to see that there are societal laws that they also accept (usually). In this stage children make moral choices because they want to be seen as being "good." Their desire to conform is fueled mostly by their desire to be seen as a good person. To a certain extent, this is still self-interest. The difference is that the relatively sophisticated cognitive capacity of older children allows them to see that someone else's opinion of them has value. Only when they develop further are they able to compare themselves to a standard that is really external. It will be later (in the postconventional level in late adolescence) before they can make moral choices based on internal moral principles.

A few years ago the law in Michigan was that when a child under the age of four was in a moving vehicle, he or she had to be in a car seat in the backseat. My wife and I were careful always to put our children in car seats, not just because it was the law, but because we wanted to keep them safe. Once, when my daughter Meredith was a few weeks away from being four years old, I had to run a short errand, and she came along. I told her to sit in the front seat and I buckled her seat belt.

"I'm sitting against the law!" she said, smiling broadly.

"Well, you're almost four so it's okay," I answered.

Her reply surprised me. "Oh, so when you're four, you can break the law whenever you want?"

Meredith was just starting to understand the idea that there were laws out there against which her behavior was to be judged and she was gleeful that she was able to do what she wanted without being caught or punished. The idea of obeying the law because it was the *right* thing to do never occurred to her because she did not yet have the mental tools to figure that out.

Moral Development and the Bible

It is with this in mind that we once again turn to our Bible stories. Imagine if these stories had nothing but flat two-dimensional characters. We would see David fighting Goliath but not weeping for Absalom. Abraham would be looking at the stars in belief but never pretending that his wife Sarah was his sister. Gideon would win the battle, but we wouldn't know that he needed reassurance from two sets of fleece. These stories could easily turn into a set of repetitive, lifeless fairytales that would do little to nurture a mature faith. But the stories in the Bible are much bigger than simple moral tales. As we have already seen, one of the wonderful things about God's Word is that the stories are about people who are much like us, making us aware that God knows what we are really like.

Faith has a number of different aspects. In his book *Teaching for Spiritual Growth*, Perry Downs suggests that faith is cognitive, relational, and volitional.[5] To help children grow in faith, he says, we need to help them know God, love God, and live the way God wants them to live. We won't accomplish any of these if we merely give them a list of dos and don'ts masquerading as stories of real people. This is one of the tensions we need to think about in planning lessons and in helping children learn the stories of the Bible. It is important that we do not reduce the Bible to a set of moral tales, while still helping our children grow up with a clear sense of right and wrong.

When we turn Bible stories into moral tales for small children, we realize that, at best, we are hoping to influence their most basic instincts and convince them that it is in their best interest to be "good." Influencing moral behavior is not the same as building faith. A church program that emphasizes moral behavior at the expense of the cognitive and relational aspects of faith is missing the point.

I think that we tend to focus a lot of our teaching on moral behavior for a couple of reasons. First of all, moral behavior is something that we can see. We know we've succeeded in teaching children how to be good if they behave themselves. A living relationship with Jesus Christ is a tougher thing to observe, but it is far more important. Second, despite being less important than a relationship with Jesus, moral behavior is important. We want our children to behave because we want them to have successful lives, we want to enjoy being around them, and it's the right thing to do. God placed within us a sense of right and wrong, and we want our children to develop that sense. Also many parents believe (whether they have actually thought it out or not) that learning to obey parents is a necessary step toward learning to obey God. Therefore we have an obligation to teach our children to obey us so that they can obey God.[6]

More than Morality

A friend of mine works in a Christian preschool that has a wonderful ministry to many parents and children who do not have a church home and have little Christian background. My friend heard one of the other teachers say that she was really trying to help the children get a sense of Christian values. She said that she saw little reason to teach children Bible stories because they would only be in a Christian setting for one year, so during the one year she wanted to teach them to make moral choices.

Being good, however, is not enough. There are plenty of people who do good things who do not have a saving knowledge of Jesus Christ. There are also plenty of Christians who make bad choices at times. In other words, Christians sin too. Fortunately, it is not our actions that bring us salvation, because salvation is the free gift of God.

We do not want to give up on helping our children live righteous lives. In James 1:22–25 we read:

> Do not merely listen to the word, and so deceive yourselves. Do what it says. Anyone who listens to the word but does not do what it says is like a man who looks at his face in a mirror and, after looking at himself, goes away and immediately forgets what he looks like. But the man who looks intently into the perfect law that gives freedom, and continues to do this, not forgetting what he has heard, but doing it—he will be blessed in what he does.

God wants what is best for us and that is to follow his law. However, as we look at the Bible, we see that there are some passages in which the inspired writer is telling us about how God wants us to live and there are other times when the writer is just telling us what happened. We need to be careful not to confuse the two and try to turn history into moralism. We want to make sure we don't minimize our faith so that it is little more than obedience to the law.

James Fowler points out that children seem to be especially open to moralizing, which he sees as a great danger. He writes that young children, those in the intuitive-projective stage (the stage that is primarily a reflection of parental faith) are in danger from the "unwitting exploitation of her or his imagination in the reinforcement of taboos and moral or doctrinal expectations."[7]

So we do indeed want our children to learn right from wrong. We also want to let the stories of the Bible shape us, but we want to do it in a way that doesn't turn the stories into only moral tales.

A Matter of Balance

Finding the balance between helping children see that the stories in the Bible apply to their lives and not moralizing is a challenge. In their book describing the Promiseland model for children's ministry, Sue Miller and David Staal list six principles that guide their lesson creation. The third principle is "Promiseland teaching is relevant and application oriented."[8] Each of their lessons answers three questions: *Know what? So what?* and *Now what?* They write, "Everyone in children's ministry will agree that application-oriented teaching is important, but the real struggle is how to make teaching relevant."[9] They go on to write, "If the *So what?* question is addressed well, children will place value on the lesson. If the answer to this question wobbles, children will not care about the lesson. Let alone remember it."[10]

Miller and Staal suggest that the story all by itself is forgettable and children will not care about the lessons it teaches. But is it necessary for adults to make an application for *every* story? This desire to have every story mean something beyond the story is perhaps a byproduct of our Western, modern Christian subculture and our distrust of anything that isn't strictly systematic. Gretchen Wolff Pritchard points out that many Christians have a weak view of metaphor. "Metaphor," she writes, "is not simply a kind of decorative language which is there to be decoded into 'concepts' or 'truths' or spiritual ideas and then discarded now that we have uncovered its essential point."[11] Often we are so intent on "getting it right," insisting on explaining all the facets of the metaphor, that we drain the metaphor of its power to grab our imagination. We also think that unless we explain it all, our students haven't really grasped the message.

It isn't just metaphor that Christians distrust, however. Some Christians seem intent on making sure that we always "get something" out of each Bible story. When we see the Bible as primarily a moral compass, it leads us to reduce stories to mere vehicles for specific lessons that help us understand the "true meaning" behind the stories. In fact some people go so far as to view Jesus's entire life as merely a set of moral lessons for us to follow. They end up seeing Jesus as *only* a great teacher. This view reduces him to a mere man—someone who happened to have wise things to say.

The Bible does shape us. Through reading it we come to know who God is, who we are, how we should live so that we please God, and many more things. But the Bible is also meant to be understood as a whole, even as we read the individual pieces. We recognize, for example, that God speaks to different people in different ways. The actions of Jael in the story of Deborah in Judges 4, when she killed Sisera by pounding a tent stake into his head, are difficult to understand in isolation. We would be reluctant to use her as a role model for young girls, but there she is in the Old Testament, celebrated as someone who saved Israel. Taking such a story out of its context in Scripture is difficult and can lead to misunderstanding. It is from its place in the whole of Scripture that each story speaks to us.

Taking a view that each story in the Bible must have a direct life application puts an unreasonable expectation on the stories. It asks the stories to represent much more than they were designed to do. In writing about Old Testament stories,

Fee and Stuart say, "Narratives are stories—purposeful stories retelling the *historical events* of the past that are intended to give meaning and direction for a given people *in the present.*"[12] "Meaning and direction" are not the same thing as moral lessons. A moral lesson is a specific application of a story. Meaning and direction are more general and speak to who we are and how we make judgments rather than how we should behave in particular situations. Fee and Stuart use helpful phrases here. They say that Old Testament stories are *historical narratives* rather than *illustrative narratives.*[13] They were not written to illustrate a specific point; they were written to tell us a bit about our history and God's work in the lives of his people.

This is true not only of Old Testament stories but of the stories of Jesus's life as well. These stories are presented so that we can learn who Jesus is. Of course there are many other lessons we can learn from the stories. When we read about Jesus touching a person with leprosy, we realize that he cared for people, even those who were considered literally untouchable. When we read about the way Jesus answered the Pharisees, we understand that he considered people more important than their strict interpretation of the law. When we read about Jesus praying in the Garden of Gethsemane, we know that he was putting our needs above his own. But if we try to look for specific moral lessons, we can find ourselves grasping at straws.

Occasionally, when our children were young, Laura and I used Bible storybooks for our family devotions at dinnertime. One particular book included the story of Jesus as a boy in the temple (Luke 2:41–50), the story of how Jesus went with his parents to celebrate Passover and was left behind when the family group began their journey home. This particular book, however, always had some sort of lesson at the end of each story. After the very brief telling of the story, the author said that Jesus went with his parents when they told him to come with them. The author used this small part of the story to form a moral lesson for the children, ending the story with: "Aren't you glad Jesus showed us how to obey our parents?" As we saw in chapter 2, there are many things in this story that we can learn, but using it as an example of how Jesus was obedient, especially when he didn't stay with his parents, just comes across as foolish.

This type of blatant moralizing suggests that the author believes just knowing about this event in Jesus's life isn't enough. It could be suggested that such a view does not trust the Holy Spirit to use the story to shape the lives of those who hear it without our making some sort of direct application. The clear implication is that without a direct connection to children's lives, the story has little value.

Letting the Story Speak

This limited view of the power of story can lead to some interesting and humorous attempts to make a lesson out of every story. Dennis Hoekstra wrote of an example of this in his monograph on religious education. In Mark 6 there is a story of adultery, manipulation, and murder. It's the story of King Herod, who married his brother's wife, Herodias. When John the Baptist spoke out against him for this, Herod had John arrested. Herodias wasn't satisfied with this punishment, however. She waited until Herod had a party and sent her daughter (extrabiblical sources tell us that her name was Salome) into the party to dance for the men. She pleased the men enough that Herod offered her anything she wanted, so she asked for the head of John the Baptist on a platter. In the curriculum that Hoekstra found, the heading and the major point of the lesson was "A Good Mother Is a Great Blessing."[14] While it is true that a good mother is a great blessing, the point of the lesson seems to have completely missed what was really going on in the story. In this case, the author's desire to moralize the story got in the way of letting the story speak for itself.

Of course there is more than one way to moralize a story. The most obvious way is to do it directly, by stating at the end of the story what the moral is. This is what we saw in the examples above. In its most direct form one hears: "and the moral of the story is . . ." just before the moral is pronounced. Often, though, moralizing is slightly less direct with a "so, boys and girls . . ." which leads into a discussion of what they should do when faced with a similar situation. For example, in the story of Jesus at the temple, you would end the telling with: "So, boys and girls, this story teaches us that it is very important that you always obey your mom and dad like Jesus did."

Another way of moralizing is to shape the story in such a way that the presentation of the characters and the events clearly suggests the moral lesson in a way that is inescapable. When the Bible storybook author ended his story about Jesus in the temple with "Aren't you glad Jesus showed us how to obey our parents?" he was giving as clear a moral as if he'd said, "So, children, obey your parents." We can clearly direct children's thoughts about a story without saying the moral in so many words.

Faith Lessons

As we think about this, it may be helpful to consider the difference between a *moral* and a *faith lesson*. A *moral* is a teaching that shows correct character or behavior. When we moralize a story, we use the story to teach how someone should behave. Moralizing a story takes the richness of a story, the intricate shadings of the decisions of the characters, the multiple ways of looking at a situation, and reduces them to one "right" way of interpreting what happened. It turns the real flesh and blood people who live in the story into flat figures who are present only to serve as either a good or bad example for us.

A *faith lesson*, on the other hand, is a reflection on the story that helps us think about who God is, who we are, or what our relationship with God is like. By being caught up in the story of Esther, for example, we can imagine ourselves in a compromising position and, after a time of personal struggle, and perhaps even a few false starts, summoning up the courage to stand up for what we believe is right. Knowing that God was with Esther helps us realize he is with us too.

The biblical story of Esther does not give a fairytale resolution. In this story the king is duped into making a decree that all Hebrews should be killed. God's solution to the problem of the king's edict was that his people would be allowed to defend themselves. This isn't a magical solution; it is a real solution to a real problem. In fact the politics of the situation made it better for the Hebrews than it would seem. By making an edict allowing the Hebrews to defend themselves, the king signals his true intentions to his soldiers and to other royals wanting to be supportive. But there was no angel appearance or sudden flash of light accompanying a miraculous resolution. This was a real-life, God-directed solution.

Reflecting on God's solution to Esther's problem and seeing how God used Esther to make it happen help us realize that God can also use us to make inroads into bad situations. *Instead of the story telling us what to do, it inspires us to think of ourselves as God's children.* Perhaps, like Esther, we might be placed in a situation so that we could do a particular task. When we wonder about how Esther felt and think about what she said, she becomes a real flesh and blood person in our mind, and this makes us realize that she is a lot like we are. In turn, it helps us be more like her, allowing us to see ourselves as people whom God can use for his purposes. When we identify with the people who live in biblical stories, the impact is more likely to cause an internal change than simply an external adjustment in our behavior.

Wondering

To help us get to know the characters in a story, we can *wonder* about them. Wondering is more than just a convenient way to end a story.[15] It is also a way that allows us to more fully understand the characters and how God worked in their lives. By wondering together with children about the story, we allow ourselves to become more emotionally invested in the story and with its characters. Wondering questions should not be a quiz to see if the children were paying attention. This isn't a chance to make sure that everyone has been with you as you told the story. In fact it has been suggested that if you already know the answer, it isn't a valid wondering question. These questions really are about wondering. They offer a chance for you and your listeners to think about the way the characters felt or the choices that they made.

For example, here are some things I wonder about in the Esther story:

- I wonder how Esther felt when she was taken to the palace for the first time. Do you think she was excited? Do you think she was scared?
- I wonder if Mordecai was afraid that he would be killed because he disobeyed Haman.
- I wonder if Esther planned on two banquets with the king and with Haman right from the start or if she got frightened at the first one and quickly decided to have a second one the next night.
- I wonder if many of the Jews died when the Babylonian soldiers came to kill them.

These questions aren't earthshaking. They aren't meant to be examples of the very best questions you can ask at the end of telling about Esther. It is actually hard to come up with wondering questions for someone else because wondering questions need to come from the teller and from the hearers. My questions may not be the things you wonder about. As you wonder about things in the story, invite the children to tell you what they wonder about.

Also these questions aren't carefully designed to get at the heart of the story. They come at the end of the story so that the storyteller and the children can spend a bit of time *living in the story*—thinking about how the people felt and thinking about what might have motivated them to do the things they did. Not only does this do justice to the story as a story and allow the storyteller and the hearers to view things from a new perspective, it also allows time to think about the particulars of the story, which means it will stay with us longer. We want the stories to stay with children so that they can be shaped by God's Word. For faith to live in children, to be part of the fabric of their lives, the stories need to be part of their thoughts and kept in their hearts. When the stories are in the hearts of our children, they can help build the three-dimensional faith that we want them to have. This won't happen as readily when we give them a list of dos and don'ts dressed up as stories.

Giving children stories populated with real people doing real things can help them in their moral development. According to Kohlberg's stages of moral development, it is natural for children to avoid punishment and to do things out of self-interest. We want to encourage them in their moral development and, through these powerful stories, help them learn about the way God wants us to live. We also want them to begin to see why the people in the stories did what they did. Those who study Kohlberg's work see that it is often the case that people do similar things for quite different reasons. Esther could have gone to the king, for example, because she was convinced that her safety was less important than the safety of her people, but she also could have gone there because she was afraid that she would be killed too. Today we may do good things for a variety of reasons. We may pay taxes, for example, because we are afraid of getting caught and fined or because it's the law and we want to obey the law. We might even pay taxes gladly because it is our way of supporting the many good things our government does on our behalf. By giving children a chance to think through what the people in these stories did and why they did them, we encourage them to think about their own lives and why they do the things they do.

Jesus talked about this in one of his parables:

> To some who were confident of their own righteousness and looked down on everybody else, Jesus told this parable: "Two men went up to the temple to pray, one a Pharisee and the other a tax collector. The Pharisee stood up and prayed about himself: 'God, I thank you that I am not like other men—robbers, evildoers, adulterers—or even like this tax collector. I fast twice a week and give a tenth of all I get.'
>
> "But the tax collector stood at a distance. He would not even look up to heaven, but beat his breast and said, 'God, have mercy on me, a sinner.'
>
> "I tell you that this man, rather than the other, went home justified before God. For everyone who exalts himself will be humbled, and he who humbles himself will be exalted."
>
> Luke 18:9–14

In this story both men were praying at the temple, but Jesus pointed out that their reasons for praying were different and that these reasons were evident in their prayers. This is true of all of us. The motivation for our actions will sometimes show up in the way we do things. It's important that our children see beyond actions and think about motivation.

This is the basis for good moral development. The irony here is that, if we really want to have an impact on the moral development of our children, we should tell them stories without morals at the end. This gives them the opportunity to consider, sometimes on their own, what people in the stories did, why they did these things, and what happened as a result. We want children to do more than just obey the law. We want to change their hearts. Helping them see the hearts of the people in the Bible stories that we tell gives them the opportunity to mature in the way they make moral decisions. And, as they focus on God's Word, it becomes more a part of their lives and encourages a faith that has depth.

7

Worship

Principle 6: Children should be part of congregational worship and they should also have opportunities to experience developmentally appropriate worship.

As we have seen, if we want our children to have the sort of three-dimensional faith that becomes part of who they are, they need to hear the stories of God, and adults need to be involved with them in a variety of ways. But should children be part of our congregational worship service or should they be in a separate program? What about teenagers? Should they be in a special youth service or should they sit with Mom and Dad?

For years either children sat in the pew with their parents, or, if they were too young, parents sat at home with the children. A separate children's ministry is a fairly recent phenomenon. Now most churches minister to infants and toddlers in a church nursery. Many churches have special worship centers for their young children. Some churches have separate worship services for their teens. In some churches parents drop their toddlers off at one place, their elementary children at another, and they watch their teens go off to their own worship center, while the adults go to the sanctuary. Sometimes this trend toward specialized ministry has resulted in splintering the family on Sunday morning.

Mark DeVries noticed this trend back in 1994 when he wrote *Family-Based Youth Ministry*. He said that traditional youth ministry has "increasingly (and often unwittingly) held to a single strategy that has become the common characteristic of this [youth ministry] model: the isolation of teenagers from the adult world and particularly from their own parents."[1] Teenagers are perhaps more often separated from adults in nonworship church settings. Churches that have a contemporary worship style have little need to make special services for teens. In fact Willow Creek Community Church in suburban Chicago, one of the churches that is in the forefront of seeker-sensitive worship, was an outgrowth of a youth program called Son City.[2] So what started as youth worship soon became worship for the whole adult congregation. But many churches provide a children's program separate from adult worship. In some of these churches the children never experience congregational worship until they are in sixth grade. In a few cases there is a separate program for middle school students, so children don't worship with their families until ninth grade.

Intergenerational Worship

We are a *community* of believers—a group who gathers weekly to worship and to serve the Lord. It is important that we do this together. In Nehemiah 8 all the people—men, women, and children—gathered together for what seems to have been a four- or five-hour worship service.

When the seventh month came and the Israelites had settled in their towns, all the people assembled as one man in the square before the Water Gate. They told Ezra the scribe to bring out the Book of the Law of Moses, which the LORD had commanded for Israel.

So on the first day of the seventh month Ezra the priest brought the Law before the assembly, which was made up of men and women and all who were able to understand. He read it aloud from daybreak till noon as he faced the square before the Water Gate in the presence of the men, women and others who could understand. And all the people listened attentively to the Book of the Law. . . .

Ezra opened the book. All the people could see him because he was standing above them; and as he opened it, the people all stood up. Ezra praised the LORD, the great God; and all the people lifted their hands and responded, "Amen! Amen!" Then they bowed down and worshiped the LORD with their faces to the ground.

Nehemiah 7:73–8:3, 5–6

The group was made up of men and women and all who were able to understand. This sounds like many of the children were there too. Should this type of intergenerational service be the model for what we do with children? Using biblical events like this as a mandate can be tricky. Just because someone in the Bible does something, it doesn't mean we all should do it. Sometimes the Bible does not explicitly state whether what is done is right or wrong. We're expected to get that from the context of the rest of the Bible. Consider, for example, much of what Samson does. We don't want our friends and family to use him as a model for modern male behavior! Even if what a person does is good, it is not necessarily the norm for us. That is to say, for example, that just because David danced in his underwear in a way that was pleasing to God (see 2 Samuel 6), we don't need to see that as a standard for our worship services. Just because Joshua led the army of Israel around Jericho seven times (see Joshua 6), we don't have to march around our city seven times. This is the challenge of reading the Bible and deciding how it should inform our lives today.[3] So just because Ezra did it that way doesn't make it the way we should do it—and no one seems to be suggesting that four-hour-long worship services are the way to go!

On the other hand we want to make sure that we don't discount the idea either. We *are* a community of faith, and corporate worship is one of the things that give us a sense of unity and of community. So how do we decide whether it is more appropriate for children to be sitting in the pew with us or off on their own in worship specifically designed for them?

Cognitive Development

One place that we can look for guidance in this area is cognitive psychology. Jean Piaget's theory focuses on cognitive development—how our thinking changes as we grow older and develop. Like all developmental theories, Piaget's stages are sequential.[4] Consequently it is not possible, for example, to do the kind of thinking that marks the fourth stage of Piaget's theory without first being able to do the kind of thinking that takes place in the third stage (see sidebar). Theorists working in other areas of development suggest that development continues on through adulthood, but Piaget notes that with regard to cognitive development, many people are in the final stage in high school.[5] This does not mean that people are finished learning at that point but they at least have the tools they need to understand abstract concepts.

Much of Piaget's theory has to do with the ability to handle abstraction. Simply put, children can't deal with abstract ideas. This has a number of implications for teachers, but it is also important for those of us concerned with children's spirituality. How can children who do not have the ability to understand abstract concepts deal with the concept of God? If they can't assemble the set of stories into a larger "story of the story," how can they make sense out of the stories from the Old and New Testaments that they hear? How can we introduce an infinite God to children who cannot understand infinity?

These are important questions to answer because they get at the very heart of our work with children. Our task is to help children understand what they can about God in such a way that they are better prepared to understand more about him when they are able. This is sometimes called "preparing a land-scape for faith." This terminology is useful because it helps us see that what we are doing with younger children has a payoff later in life in their faith walk. At the same time we do not want to minimize the faith that children have. Many children can and do have faith, but their ability to think about and express their faith is different from that of adults.

Piaget's Theory of Cognitive Development

Sensorimotor Stage—ages 0–2. Children begin to make use of imitation, memory, and thought. They move from doing things merely by reflex to thinking about actions and then doing them.

Preoperational Stage—ages 2–7. The use of language and the ability to think through things logically begin to develop. Children at this stage continue to have difficulty seeing things from another person's point of view.

Concrete Operational Stage—ages 7–11. Children are able to solve hands-on problems in a logical manner. They are able to classify things and put them in order.

Formal Operational Stage—ages 11–adult. Children are now able to solve abstract problems and are able to think scientifically and show concern for social issues and personal identity.

Applying Cognitive Development to Church Programs

How does this translate into the actual nuts and bolts of children's programs in churches? We need to determine if children can handle the adult-oriented material that is presented in congregational worship or if they should have their own worship experiences. Many writers, even those who are proponents of separate worship for children, have expressed a desire for children and adults to worship together. Two of the people who were instrumental in the start of the Children's Worship movement, Sonja Stewart and Jerome Berryman, write that their first choice is to have all ages worshiping together.[6] They admit that their children's worship model is a compromise, perhaps because adults are not willing to work hard enough to make worship accessible for children.

Others go further and suggest that worship should be *the* integrating activity for churches. Karen Wilk writes that worship is the place, much like a family meal, where all the members gather.

> Consider for a moment how we approach meals. Most of our meals are family affairs: young, old, and in-between gather around the table, and the food and conversation cater to all ages in varying degrees throughout the dining experience. It is a family event, and everyone is included and everyone participates. Of course there are special occasions such as a dinner party for adults or a child's birthday party when one age group is the center of attention, but these are the exceptions. The regular fare sustains and supports every family member on a regular basis.[7]

Perhaps a family meal is a good model to consider. At my house when my family gathers for a meal, my wife and I sit down with our four children and, as we eat, we talk about things of interest to the family and of the things that are going on in our lives. But there is more to the meal than this. When the meal is over and it is time for our family devotions, we make a choice. When our children were younger, we had to choose between devotions in which young children were engaged or a devotional time aimed at the older children. We could have chosen just to read long passages from Scripture, but most of what our children would have learned from this was to sit quietly and find other ways to occupy their minds until it was over. Bible storybooks or children's devotionals aim at the cognitive level of young children. Adult or teen books use words and discuss concepts that young children can't understand, because their cognitive level does not yet allow them to deal with abstract concepts.[8] So the problem wasn't a matter of preferences; it was about *what children are able to understand.*

Making Congregational Worship Child Friendly

In our family devotions we chose material that took into account the cognitive differences of our children, and the same must be done in worship services. We want to accept and rejoice in our children for who they are. Because they are part of our faith community, we desire to have our children join us for worship, but we also want to honor their cognitive differences. We can do this in two ways, by involving children in the worship service and by providing separate worship opportunities for them.

Involving Children in Worship

First of all, we want our children to relate to, understand, and participate in many parts of the worship service. There are two ways children can be involved in the service—as active

103

participants in worship leadership and as active participants in the pew.

One way to include children as worship leaders is to have them participate in some of the ritual that takes place in the service. Children are able to help in these parts because the ritual remains relatively unchanged and children learn how to do the tasks quite well. As I mentioned in chapter 2, our church has a candle that is lit at the beginning of each service and, during the singing of one of the opening songs two third graders walk down the center aisle, one to light the candle and the other carrying the Bible. They bring the light and the Word forward, light the candle, and place the Bible on the pulpit. The children have gotten very good at doing this. We bought sashes for the children to wear, which adds to the ceremonial nature. The third graders take this task very seriously and they do it well. Sometimes the candle is too tall for the child to light, and the pastor helps him or her. The image of a young boy or girl lighting the candle with the pastor in his robe helping is a wonderful picture of intergenerational worship.

This experience adds to the children's worship, and the children feel that they play an important role in the church. We always use third graders to do this because in this grade they are studying how the church worships as a congregation, so it makes sense to give them a specific part in the service. By now all the children in our church know that this is a third grade task. The younger children look forward to having the opportunity to light the candle and bring the Bible up the aisle when they are in third grade.

For this to work successfully, it is important for the adults in our church to be thoughtful concerning the needs of the children in planning for their participation. The children aren't left on their own; an adult takes the responsibility to be at the back of church with the lighter, the sash, and the Bible to help the children get started. The children are willing to participate because they trust the adults to do things in a way that makes them feel comfortable with the setting and with their task.

There are other ways to have children involved in worship. They can do special readings or participate in presentations. Sometimes children are reluctant to do these things because they aren't confident of their reading ability. Children can find some of the readings challenging, even if they're not reading Scripture. It is important to ask children to read or participate in ways that allow them to succeed and to feel good about what they have done. When writing something for children to read in church, use vocabulary that they won't stumble over and make each part short enough for children to read with confidence. Children do best when reading only two or three sentences at a time. They feel less pressure and thus are more confident. Having short readings also allows you to involve more children.

An example of writing that is specifically for children is the drama in appendix A. We wanted to present the first missionary journey of Paul in a way that could help the congregation better understand what happened. We decided to use our middle school students to present the information in a readers' theater. Notice how, even though there is a lot of information presented, no one student has to speak a lot of dialogue at any one time. Because we wrote the drama with short and easy lines, the students felt more at ease about participating. We were careful to include vocabulary that was familiar to the students, even though there were some names of cities they had to practice a little.

When writing your own plays and presentations, pay attention to the length of the parts and the vocabulary. If using someone else's writings, don't be afraid to rewrite things so that your children can read them more easily.

It is also helpful to have children practice—but not too much. We want children to do well when they lead us in worship. If they do poorly, the congregation will be focusing on the children and not on worship, plus the children won't feel good about the experience and will be reluctant to do it again. But we need to resist the temptation to practice things to death. Give the children the readings a week ahead of time and ask them to read it out loud with their parents one time every evening. Then go over it with them in your worship space so that they feel comfortable with the microphone or with the podium. That's probably enough. Multiple practices with high pressure are only going to make children dread participating in worship. If you relax, they will too.

One can participate in worship, of course, without being a leader. There are a variety of resources with ideas for helping children feel as though they are part of a worship service.[9] Making the congregational worship service more understandable can play an important part. The language that is used in the bulletin for the order of worship can be intimidating for children (and for visitors). One church in my community has tried to go out of their way to make sure that the language they use is understandable. This can be really helpful.

When I was a child, I attended a church with an order of worship in the bulletin that was handed out as we entered church and sat in the pew. I noticed that at the beginning of each worship service my bulletin read "Votum and Salutation." As a child the only thing I knew about these words was that they were written at the beginning of the worship service in the bulletin. The pastor never spoke these words. He said some other things that were like a prayer. He also brought us God's greeting by raising his hands. But he never said "votum" or "salutation." That phrase in the bulletin was not helpful to me as a child or to many adults. A friendlier way of noting this would be to use the words "Opening prayer" and "God's greeting," which say much the same thing but in a more familiar way.

We don't want to reduce our worship to the lowest common denominator (what some might call "dumbing down our worship"), and we don't want to take all the elegance and beauty out of the language, but we do need to be aware that there is a balance we can reach. We may rarely hear phrases like "Votum and Salutation" in church today, but "intercessory prayer" or even "confession and assurance" are going to confuse children and leave them thinking that church is something for older people.

The point of all this is that by being aware of the presence of children and having a desire to involve them in worship, we can adjust our language so that the time that we spend together is valuable to all of us. It is important, though, for us to remember that some things that are valuable for adults are not going to be understood by children. This poses a dilemma. Do we ignore adults so that the whole service is child friendly? Do we ignore children and hope that they'll figure it out at some point? Neither of these solutions seems right. If both adults and children are members of the community, we ought to be able to find a way to address the needs of both.

There are important parts of a worship service for which children are just not ready. Usually it's not hard to figure out which parts these are. Sometimes you can just watch the children in your church and see what is connecting and what isn't. One child who helps us figure it out is Mason. Mason has been interested in what goes on in church for a long time—well, a long time for Mason, since he's only five. For years, though, he has shown a real interest in things related to church and to faith. On a recent Sunday, after a relatively short pastoral prayer, Mason turned around and looked at my high school–aged daughter and said, "He prays too long!"

Mason is a joy to many of us in our church programs since he responds with such enthusiasm. But if Mason isn't engaged, there is a good chance that other children are not either. How can we help Mason and other children like him worship in ways that meet their unique cognitive needs? In addition to making our worship service more accessible to children, we should create special worship opportunities for them. Therefore, we need a twofold approach to worship with children. Not only should we worship together, we should also worship separately.

Providing Separate Worship for Children

A twofold approach for making worship real for children can help them feel like a valued part of the community while at the same time addressing their unique cognitive needs. Many churches, including the one in which I worship, try to help children feel like a part of our community by having those who are three years old through third grade worship with their parents for the first ten to fifteen minutes of our service. During this time we typically have an opening song, we hear God's greeting, we confess our sins, and we hear that God forgives us. We encourage parents to engage their children in this part of the service by helping them find songs in the hymn book, pointing out what is going on in the bulletin, and other things. During the singing of a song, the children are dismissed for children's worship.

Some children need one of their parents to walk out of church with them to help them feel secure in the worship center, and congregations need to help parents feel free to leave the worship service to do this. The moving in and out of the service can be distracting, but if we want to build a community that truly accepts children, it is crucial to encourage parents both to care for their children and to participate in worship.

Parents may have less of a need to go with their children if there are people whose task it is to watch the children as they move from congregational worship to children's worship. When the children see the same familiar faces at the back of the sanctuary every week, they feel quite comfortable taking the adult's hand and going to the worship center. It is important that parents feel that their children are being watched and are cared for during this transition time. If the parents are comfortable with the care their children are receiving, they are able to more fully participate in congregational worship.

The Children in Worship Model

A popular program of worship for children is Children and Worship, developed by Sonja Stewart and Jerome Berryman. Berryman's ideas came from his work with Sofia Cavaletti who, in turn, incorporated ideas and methods she learned from Maria Montessori.

When I first became aware of the work of Stewart and Berryman, they helped me see that faith nurture is more than just education. Though worship sometimes contains a healthy education component, the traditional Sunday school is all about education—it is school with a sacred subject. Worship is different. The beauty of the model that Young Children in Worship represents is that we can worship *with* children in what is sometimes called the "catechesis of the Good Shepherd."

This particular style of worship with children uses a litany that recalls some of the most ancient litanies. For example, they open worship with "The Lord be with you" to which children respond "and also with you." In addition to being spoken, they use signing to add a kinesthetic dimension to the words, which makes this more of a whole-body experience for the children—and also for the adult leaders. The ancient words of the *shema* are spoken to each other, "Hear, O Israel, the Lord our God, the Lord is one."

Children in these worship centers listen to the stories of faith, told in a remarkable way, with figures either made of stiff laminated paper, which are carefully moved on the floor, or with wooden figures that stand up. The use of these figures helps the storyteller and the children focus on the story as an entity in and of itself. At the end of the story, which is usually told very simply, the worship leader helps the children wonder about the story, similar to my examples in chapter 6. "I wonder," she says, after telling a story about Noah, "how God got all the animals to the ark." "I wonder how Noah felt when God asked him to build this boat and there was no rain to be seen." We invite the children to wonder with us, bringing them into a discussion of the story, being careful not to turn the story into a fable with a moral lesson tacked on the end.

After this time of wondering, the children are invited to respond to what they have heard. They have a number of ways to do this, from working with art materials to retelling the story using the wooden or paper figures as the leader did. There are some musical instruments available as well as a "prayer corner" where children can go by themselves. This is a time that gives the children a chance to reflect on the story while keeping themselves busy and occupied in childlike activities. After the response time, the children gather again in the circle to share what they have done, to pray, and to receive a parting blessing.

This type of worship has been beneficial for both the children and the leaders in our church. Children first enter this program with a scaled-down version for three-year-olds and continue through second grade. Our children's leadership team was especially pleased that our church was willing to incorporate some items from the worship centers in congregational worship. For example, in children's worship we talked about the seasons of the church year, something that our congregation had not historically paid much attention to. That was added to congregational worship. Even with this help we felt that we needed to do a better job of helping children make the connection between what they saw and heard in congregational worship with what was going on in children's worship.

We created a curriculum for third graders in which we used a similar litany to what was used in the worship center with the other children, but we used more complex stories and added a component of talking directly about worship. In this curriculum we outline the different parts of a worship service for the children and speak specifically about the activities in our worship centers that are similar to parts of congregational worship.

Third grade children meet in the worship center about half as often as the younger children do. On the weeks that children's worship does not meet, we give the children a sheet, stapled to the church's worship folder, with questions for the children to think about during or before the congregational worship service. Usually the questions direct the children to think about some specific areas of worship that we mentioned in the worship center the week before. For example, we might ask them to look in the bulletin to see where our collection money is going this week. We might give them small sticky-notes and ask them to mark the songs in the hymnbook that we will be singing during the worship service. These "third grade thinking pages" are designed to help the children, along with their parents, think about how the different parts of the worship service are put together and how they are like what the children have been doing for years in the worship centers. An example of one thinking page, in which we asked children to draw what they were hearing in the sermon, is shown here. We had discussed the sermon the week before. This shows how well one of our third graders, Isla, listened to the sermon and was able to communicate through pictures what the pastor said.

Another idea that we have found helpful in all our children's worship centers is to use middle school students as helpers.

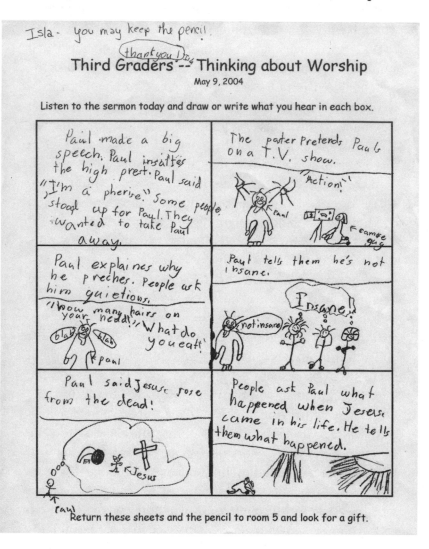

These older children are always at the door of each worship center ready to greet the children by name. This allows us to make sure that any visitors are greeted individually and that parents who are visiting can see where their children are going to be and with whom. This may seem like a small thing, but we believe that this is one way of sending a message to parents and to children that they are safe at our church.

Some people criticize the Young Children in Worship model, saying that we ought to keep the children in the congregational worship service, adjusting it so that it is more accessible to children. As you can see from the first part of this chapter, I agree that this is an important and necessary part of building faith in children, but it has been my experience that *just* adjusting congregational worship for children is difficult for a number of reasons. The biggest reason is that much of what we do in worship is cognitive—it depends on our ability to understand abstract ideas. Adults want to hear sermons that challenge them intellectually as well as spiritually, and we want to give adults this experience in worship. Prayers can be long in congregational worship, and for many children this will be a time for wiggling and paying attention to anything but the prayer. A lot of what we do in worship can and should be aimed at our adult members. It is helpful to both the children and the adults to have other, appropriate worship experiences for children at the same time.

Congregations may try to address the needs of children by adjusting congregational worship, but it is difficult to do this on an ongoing basis. The simple fact is that planning good worship is hard and planning good worship while keeping children in mind makes it even harder. Most congregations aren't able to do it fifty-two weeks a year.

Worship is the defining event for most congregations. It is a time when, as a people of God, a community of faith, we join together to meet God. In his book *Vision and Character: A Christian Educator's Alternative to Kohlberg*, Craig Dykstra makes this point well. He writes:

> Worship is not "mere" symbol or ritual. These symbolic actions have a way of training us and shaping us at precocious levels so that over time their order becomes embedded in us. In worship we see and sense who it is we are to be and how it is we are to move in order to become. Worship is an enactment of the core dynamics of the Christian life. This is why worship is its central and focusing activity. It is paradigmatic for all the rest of the Christian life.[10]

For children to have the kind of faith that we want them to have, they need to be part of a worship experience. They need to see their parents and their parents' friends gathered in worship. By seeing the adults who are important to them gathered to meet God, they see the church and they see that they have a place in it. They observe the gathering of a people whose faith is rich and whose lives reflect the truth of the stories that they have been told in children's worship, in church school, and in their homes. They become aware that these people have their own stories, stories that help the children of the church know that God still works today in the lives of people just as he did in the time of the Bible stories. If we want our children to grow in faith, we have to give them opportunities to worship with the entire congregation and also to worship in ways that are developmentally appropriate. They need both.

8

Creating a
Child-Friendly Culture

In any church an effective way to help children's faith grow is to create a culture in which children are valued and accepted. This type of culture, one in which people understand that children are an important part of the community, integrates children into the full life of the church and makes a church three-dimensional-faith friendly. Such a culture enables children to grow in their faith, not necessarily through listening to sermons but through seeing that the faith of the people in the congregation lives deep inside of them. When the people of the church are thinking about children, many of them, not just the children's ministries director or Sunday school superintendent, will want to make things happen for children.

Growing a church that has this sort of attitude can take years, depending on what the church is like to begin with, but there are things you can do to help encourage the formation of such a culture. In this chapter I suggest some good ways to start.

Involving All the Children

Go out of your way to make sure to include all the children whenever you can. If you have children light the candle in church, make a schedule that shows that all the children will have a turn. If you hand out rhythm instruments during singing, make sure that every child gets one. If you present a church school Christmas program, make sure that all of the children have a part. If you come up one or two parts short, rewrite the play to include more people.

When Laura and I plan the children's Christmas programs in our church, we write our own programs and create them in such a way that there is no main character.[1] No one child stands out as the star. We go so far as to count the lines (because we know that some of the kids will!) to make sure that the parts are about even. If they aren't, we rewrite the play to make sure that each of the children feels good about his or her part. No one child has the lead role.[2] The Christmas program and other such activities should be used to build community not to cause problems. If the children have lived for a while with a system that promotes fairness, they come to expect it, and often they won't complain when they aren't chosen to do something because they know their turn will come.

Providing Authentic Tasks

As we saw in chapter 2, another way to build a child-friendly culture is to give children and teens authentic tasks in the church. In this case, *authentic* means that they are tasks that truly need to be done, are seen as having value, and are tasks over which the children can take ownership. The example of children lighting the candle is a fine example. With minimal support these third graders perform this task on their own and they take pride in it. They do it well and support each other.

At one church the person in charge of the sound system needed help and had the wonderful idea of asking some of the older middle school boys to assist him. Two of them jumped at the chance and, whenever they could, they sat back by the soundboard learning the ropes. It didn't take long before they were able to handle things on their own and now take real ownership of the sound system. They show up early for services, set up for special events, and love a complex service, so they can work hard and serve. Along the way they have learned about worship, about service, and about mentoring. Now they have asked a couple of younger boys to assist them.

Using middle school students as helpers in children's worship is something that worked well for our church. We made a point of meeting with the middle school students early in the year to talk about what their role would be in the worship center. We explained that we needed them to be role models for the younger children in helping them worship. The seventh and eighth graders who were involved took their role seriously because we did. We listed their names in the church bulletin along with the adult leader. Of course some of these young teens do better than others, but we are often surprised at how they rise to the occasion and are more mature than we might have expected.

One of the benefits of giving young people authentic tasks is that they feel empowered to do other important things in the church. When our midweek boys and girls clubs needed additional leaders, the teens who had been working with younger children for two years asked if they could be leaders. They had established relationships with the younger children in our church, which helped them become involved at the very center of church life instead of being relegated to the periphery.

I remember sitting at pinewood derby night, a night when our boys and girls race small wooden cars, which they have made in their clubs, on a long wooden track at our church. Over the years it has become a whole-church affair with refreshments and lots of people coming to watch and join the fun. As I sat watching some of the races, I saw my seventeen-year-old son, Bryan, who was a boys club leader, sitting on the other side of the track with a sixth grader next to him and a four-year-old on his lap. They were enjoying the races together. Because Bryan had already had an opportunity to build big-brother-type relationships with these younger boys, he became a role model for them as well as a friend.

Don't create tasks just to keep young people busy and don't ask teens to do the things that the adults don't want to do. Children and teens have a well-developed sense of fairness and, if it seems to them that they are being asked to do things that are not really helpful, they will see it. Sometimes well-meaning adults suggest that young people can do tasks that the adults don't want to do. If the church grounds need work or if an old carpet needs to be torn up, we may hear, "Maybe we can get the young people to do it."

There is a difference between allowing children and young people to be authentically involved in the life of the church and dumping on them jobs that no one else wants to do. Listen to children and young people. They will reveal what things help them feel like valued members of the church.

Thinking about What Children Will Do

Many, perhaps even most, church events are planned by and for adults. Even things that are supposed to be intergenerational are sometimes not really geared for children. One church I know will have some of their congregational meetings (at which they discuss a new building project or select church lay leadership) after the morning worship service. They ask a few adults to show a *Veggie Tales* or some other video to keep the children busy. The children have already been sitting for quite some time (church school meets before worship at this church), so asking the children (even the older ones) to sit still for another half hour is really unfair.

When Saddleback Church produced materials so that churches could spend forty days going through the book *The Purpose Driven Life*, many churches made a point of creating materials for children as well. In our church the committee who ran the program invited teens and children to meet with the small group discussions. Younger children went with their parents, but teens were in groups with other adults. After an opening time with all group members, one of the adults took the children to a different part of the house in which the group met and worked through some age-appropriate materials with them. Afterward the children showed the adult group what they had done in their own session.

Not everything has to be special or different. At a recent all-church square dance, one church made sure they included children in the invitation and many of the squares included five- and six-year-olds, and they were not always in groups with their parents. These examples show that people are taking the time to think about children and to create opportunities for them to be actively engaged.

Helping Children Look for the Sacred in the Ordinary

To help children and teens build a faith that goes beyond the surface, we need to help them realize that they can see God in many things. God is the Creator of the universe and the whole world belongs to him. Their life with God isn't restricted to just Sunday mornings or times when they're in church. It also can't be restricted to just times when we mention Jesus by name. There are many places that we can see God's work and there are many people who point to God in their writing, speaking, music, or art. By helping children see that God is part of the everyday lives of these people, they can begin to see that God is involved in all parts of their lives as well.

Children's literature can help them understand that God is a part of their whole life. In appendix B there is a bibliography of a large number of books that Laura and I have used with children in our church. Some of these books talk directly about God but others do not. *The Lotus Seed* and *All the Places to Love* are two examples of books that, on the surface, do not have much to do with faith but have been used with children to help them see that faith has an impact on everything that happens—not just what happens in church.

The Lotus Seed by Sherry Garland, illustrated by Tatsuro Kiuchi, is a wonderfully told and illustrated story of a woman from Vietnam who is forced to leave her home and her country and to settle in the United States. When, as a young woman, she sees the emperor cry in his garden as he loses his throne, she sneaks down to take a lotus seed from the garden to remember the emperor by. This lotus seed becomes very important to her. She has it in her pocket when she is married, and when she has to leave Vietnam in a hurry and can take little with her, she takes the lotus seed. Many years later she shows the seed to her grandchildren and tells them the story of how she got it. One of her grandchildren, curious about what a lotus plant would look like, takes the seed and plants it somewhere in the onion patch; he's not even sure where. His grandmother is very upset with her grandson.

One day the grandmother looks out the window and sees a lotus blossom unfurling its petals in the garden. She gathers her grandchildren around the flower, and when the flower becomes a pod, she gives each of her grandchildren a lotus seed to remember her by and she keeps one for herself to remember the emperor by.

This book does not appear to have anything particularly spiritual about it (except the brief mention that the grandmother has a family altar). In fact the lotus blossom is a symbol used by many Buddhists, but in our worship centers the book can reveal to the children the image of death and resurrection. If they wish to talk about it, we tell them that the flower reminds us that Jesus died and rose again, kind of like the flower did.

The granddaughter is the narrator in this story, and she ends the book by saying that someday she will show her seed to her children and tell them about the day her grandmother saw the emperor cry. The idea of wanting to share something important that we hold close to our heart with our children and with others is a valuable concept for children to grasp.

This same idea is the basis of another wonderful book, *All the Places to Love* by Patricia MacLachlan, illustrated by Michael Wimmer. In this book the narrator is Eli, a young boy who lives on a farm with his mama and papa and his grandmother and grandfather. Ever since Eli was old enough to listen, all four adults have told Eli the things they love about the place where they live. Throughout the book Eli tells about his mama's favorite place (the blueberry barren), his papa's favorite place (the fields), his grandmother's favorite place (the stream), and his grandfather's favorite place (the barn). In the barn the grandfather has carved in a rafter his name, his wife's name, the names of Eli's mama and papa, and Eli's name. When Eli's new sister, Sylvie, is born, Eli and his grandfather carve Sylvie's name into the rafter next to the others, and Eli says he will show Sylvie all the places to love and recounts what his grandmother, grandfather, mother, and father have told him about what they love best about the land on which they live. Then Eli adds his own special place to the list and plans to tell Sylvie about that too.

The image of the family names being carved into the rafter is one that sticks with me and also with children as we read this book together. I don't know if MacLachlan had faith in mind as she wrote this book, but this image is much like the family of God. As soon as we are born, our names are added to the book of the church family, there with the names of our parents and perhaps our grandparents. If we had an actual book or perhaps if we used the rafters in the church building, we could also see the names of people who have been members of our church who have passed away and have gone to heaven. This picture book gives us an opportunity to talk with children about how they are not potential members of our church but that they are already members of our church and of God's family.

Helping students see that there are glimpses of God and of his people in literature like this will help them see that their faith in God stretches beyond the walls of their church or even the borders of their city. If we want our children to have a faith that reaches deep inside of them and becomes part of who they are, we need to help them realize that God is in the hearts and minds of people, sometimes even when they're not using his name.

Offering Developmentally Appropriate Activities

As we saw in chapter 7, children think differently than adults do because their cognitive ability is not the same. This fact should be considered whenever planning activities for children, including the children's sermon.

At some point in the service in many churches, children are called up to the front of the sanctuary, often asked to sit on the floor or perhaps on the steps leading up to the platform, and the pastor or a layperson delivers a children's sermon. One popular type of children's sermon is the object lesson, when the speaker holds up some object and makes a connection between the object and God or between the object and the Christian life. For example, the speaker might hold up a glass or a cup and say that we are like this cup, because God pours blessings into us so much that it overflows. The speaker might even fill the cup to overflowing. It is indeed true that God blesses us in ways that we cannot understand or comprehend. The image of the overflowing cup is scriptural. In Psalm 23:5 we read: "You prepare a table before me in the presence of my enemies. You anoint my head with oil; my cup overflows."

The image of the cup overflowing is a good one that communicates well to many of us but not necessarily to children. The cup representing us and the water in the cup representing the blessings of God are pretty abstract ideas that young children do not have the cognitive tools to understand. Many times our teaching requires abstract thought. We would serve our children well if we were more careful about the things we ask them to consider. In her book *Sharing the Easter Faith with Children*, Carolyn Brown has done a fine job of laying out what children can understand in the Easter story. Brown actually goes through different aspects of Easter and considers children of different ages and how they can best understand the message of this celebration in a way that makes sense to them. In considering three-, four-, and five-year-olds, for example, Brown notes: "three- through five-year-olds (preschoolers) are ready to hear more detailed accounts of the Holy Week events. To the Palm Sunday parade, they can add the stories of the Last Supper, the very basics of Jesus' crucifixion and burial, and the story of Mary at the empty tomb. Feelings continue to be the most important interpreters of the story."[3]

Learning what children can understand at various ages is essential for the success of many aspects of our church ministry, not just children's sermons. I remember many years ago seeing my three-year-old twins standing in front of the church, singing, "I will make you fishers of men" with all their hearts. What made it especially fun was that they made a motion like they had a fishing pole and they were casting their line out every time they sang the word "fishers." It was cute, the children enjoyed singing, and the congregation appreciated what they added to the worship.

After the service I asked Bryan what the song was about. "It's about fishing," he said proudly, convinced that he had paid attention and that he knew the right answer. He did know the right answer, at least as much as we could expect a three-year-old to know. This points to the need for us to think about the developmental level of children and what they are able to comprehend so that we can minister to them most effectively. There are lots of cute songs that children can really understand. We should make a point of using them.

Encouraging Adults to Spend Time with Children and Teens

Perhaps the single most important thing you can do to help your church give children a three-dimensional faith is to encourage adults to spend time with the children and teens in your congregation. Through relationships, children and teens learn what it means to live for the Lord. In his book *Transforming Children into Spiritual Champions*, George Barna writes, "Young people admit to being highly influenced by their role models and to be actively seeking more such examples, but nearly half of all preteens (44 percent) admit that they don't have any role models."[4]

There are lots of examples of how adults can build relationships with children. At our church, at the end of each summer, our youth leader calls older church members and asks them to be a prayer partner for a middle or high school student. If possible, teens and adults continue with their same prayer partners for as long as they are both available. In many cases this will go on for the six years that the students are in middle and high school. The quality of these relationships varies, of course, with some partners connecting on a deep personal level and others not. (This is the reason we need more than this way for young people and adults to connect.)

Our youngest daughter, Lynnae, has been greatly blessed by her prayer partner. Recently Lynnae wrote about this person in her blog.[5] Here is some of what she wrote: "So, when I was in the 7th grade at my church we all got assigned prayer partners. You have the same one until you go to College, and I thought that it would be really kind of stupid. I mean the prayer partners are all old people and they take you out like once every 2 months and I thought that it would be really boring. And for another thing, I know people who didn't really have a good time with their prayer partners. But my prayer partner is really cool.

"Her name is Mary and every time I talk to her she is getting ready to go on a trip to some other country. She always sends me postcards from the places she goes. I really like that because I would love to travel all over the world like she does.

And for another thing she always finds things that I really like to do. Like for instance, tonight we are going to see the local college production of *Oliver*. I am really excited because I have always wanted to see that musical.

"Every time I talk to her I find out something new about her. Like that her husband was a famous Christian Writer and she adopted a kid and the kid got leukemia and passed away from it. She is really fun to talk to."

As you can see, Mary made a real impact on Lynnae. Earlier this year Lynnae had to do an assignment for school in which she had to write about someone, not in her family, who had an impact on her faith. She chose to write about Mary. She called Mary and the two of them went out for ice cream so Lynnae could ask her questions about her faith and her life. The two of them talked and talked about what Mary's life had been like, about hardships that she had faced, and how her faith had helped her get through it all. Lynnae learned about what it means to have a faith that is strong, that can impact every part of her life, and she saw it in a friend and fellow church member who is old enough to be retired.

Other young people have felt this kind of support in their church too. One young woman, who went on to study and lead worship in college, wrote about how the support she got from her church had an impact on her: "I gained confidence as a musician from a very young age, singing and playing the violin in church with my family and with my friends. If it wasn't for the friendliness of my church I might never have had the courage to sing in public, or to play violin without music in front of me. And if it wasn't for the encouragement of church members, I might not have had the confidence to continue to develop those gifts elsewhere. Now, leading worship musically is among the most fulfilling things I do. The community is more important there than perfection, so out-of-tune violin duets, pre-adolescent singing groups, and hesitant readings are all treasured as bringing what we have to the glory of God. And as we grow up, these childish offerings become more mature gifts, partly because of experience and practice.

"My church is where I learned what real community looks like, and what it means to be in a church family. It is where I learned how I can use my gifts for God's work. I was given examples of how to bring God our best, and I've been shown how God can use our meager efforts to God's glory. The person I am today was in many ways shaped by the church I grew up in."

The importance of adults spending time with children and teens cannot be overemphasized. As the pace of our lives continues to get faster and as many families find it more difficult to spend time together, it is vital that we remember what we learned in chapter 2, that children need the guidance of a whole community of faith. The most effective way to communicate a three-dimensional faith to our children is not to do it in isolation; we need each other.

Stewards of the Mysteries

We have been entrusted with the secret things of God. We are the stewards of the mysteries. We have been blessed with a glimpse of who God is and how he is a part of our lives, and we have a wonderful opportunity to share this knowledge with our children. We want more for our children than just a knowledge of God, though. We also want them to love him and desire to serve him. We want them to have his Word deep in their hearts so that, in every part of their lives, they have Jesus Christ at the center.

Faith does indeed come from God, but he has given us an important role in helping our children come to know him. Through gathering our resources as a church family, we can have an impact on the way that children view God and their relationship to him. Through paying attention to what we can learn from the Bible and from those who have studied children, we can have church programs that help to build three-dimensional faith in our children. It is one of the most important things we can do.

Appendix A

Traveling with Paul

Bringing the First Missionary Journey to Life

ROBERT J. KEELEY, LAURA KEELEY,
AND MARVIN J. HOFMAN

Keeping Paul's missionary journeys straight can be tough. The
stories are brief and many involve mostly preaching. It is hard to
remember what happened. Our challenge was to communicate
the information about Paul's first missionary journey to our congregation in a way that was interesting, memorable, and brief. We
wanted to present information about cities as well as people.

To do this we wrote the following dramatic presentation.
Some of our characters represented cities while others represented specific people—Paul, Barnabas, and John Mark. The
students representing cities held signs on six-foot poles with
the names of the cities on them so it was very clear which city
each student represented. The three missionaries were able to
move from city to city to tell us what they did in each place.

We asked our 6th–8th grade students to read the parts because we want children of all ages to participate in worship whenever possible and 6th–8th graders are old enough to read well without a lot of practice. They read their parts as they stood at one of three microphones set up across the front of our sanctuary. We have the ability to use PowerPoint in our sanctuary and we prepared a slideshow with maps and a timeline of Paul's life up to his first journey.

The main focus, though, was on the middle school students who presented the journey. The readers *represented* the cities and the missionaries rather than played their parts. This allowed us to have them talk about the cities and the missionaries in the third person while it still gave us the opportunity to show those representing Paul, Barnabas, and John Mark moving from one microphone to the other, representing the journey from one city to the next. Also, since we believe it is important whenever possible to use *all* the children of a certain age group, this allowed us to use either boys or girls to represent the male missionaries.

Note that even though the Bible refers to Paul as Saul at the beginning of this journey and changes to Paul in the middle of it, we used only the name Paul because we thought there were already plenty of names in this short presentation without one character being referred to in two different ways. You will notice that most of the cities are represented by one reader but Antioch of Syria is read by two. This was done to add variety to what could be an otherwise long batch of information about Antioch but also we wanted the number of readers to match the number of students we had involved. Others who use this drama should combine or split parts to match the needs of their church.

This drama was given as part of the sermon during a Sunday evening service. To set the stage for the lesson to come, we had a classic painting of Paul shown on the screen as the congregation entered. After a time of singing and prayer, we turned our attention to Paul's first journey. As an introduction to our drama, the pastor said a few words about the life of Paul. We used the picture of Paul as a backdrop for the introductory comments and for the short sermon after the drama. The dates and descriptions shown below were projected onto the screen, and the congregation heard a brief overview of what brought Paul to the point in his life where he was ready to go out and preach to people in other parts of the world. The 6th, 7th, and 8th graders were then invited forward to present the drama. When we moved from city to city in the drama, arrows appeared on the map that we projected to help the congregation better understand where Paul and his companions were at each stage of the journey.

Important Dates in Paul's Life

AD 5	Born in Tarsus
35	Converted on the road to Damascus
35–38	Ministers in Arabia and Damascus (Gal. 1:17)
38	Visits Jerusalem (Gal. 1:18)
38–43	Ministers in Syria and Cilicia (Gal. 1:21)
43–46	Serves in Antioch with Barnabas
47–49	First missionary journey (Acts 13–14)

Paul's First Missionary Journey

City 1—Antioch of Syria

Antioch 1 and Antioch 2 stand holding a sign that reads Antioch. Paul, Barnabas, and John Mark are standing next to them, each with a sign that states who they are.

Antioch 1: Antioch of Syria is the third largest city in the Roman Empire. There are about sixty-four cities named Antioch in this area. Many, like Antioch of Syria, are named after famous leaders. Antioch of Syria was named by the Syrian general Seleucus, around 300 BC, after his father, Antiochus.

Antioch 2: In 64 BC Antioch was captured by the great Roman general Pompey.

Antioch 1: Antioch of Syria was full of magnificent temples to various gods. The god Apollo promoted pagan worship and immoral practices. Because these people paid so much attention to these gods, many in the city were open to new religious thoughts.

Antioch 2: A number of Jews settled here after the Syrian and Babylonian captivity. Followers of Christ also came here after the stoning of Stephen, when they were fleeing the persecution in Jerusalem. The gospel was gladly received and a church began to meet here. Barnabas and Paul taught the new believers in Antioch for a whole year.

Paul: Antioch is probably best known now as the place where believers in Jesus were first called Christians. The church in Antioch sent Paul, Barnabas, and John Mark to Cyprus and Asia Minor as missionaries.

Barnabas: John Mark later went on to write the Gospel of Mark.

John Mark: It was here that Paul's first missionary journey began. Paul, Barnabas, and John Mark traveled from Antioch to Cyprus.

City 2—Cyprus

Paul, Barnabas, and John Mark walk to the person with the Cyprus sign.

Cyprus: Cyprus is an island in the Mediterranean Sea not far from the Syrian coast. Over the years Philistines and

Phoenicians settled here. Cyprus became a province of Rome after Pompey conquered the region.

Antioch 1: Hey, that's the same guy that captured Antioch in 64 BC.

Cyprus: Yes, it is. Both places became part of the Roman Empire. Travel from place to place was now easier than before—it was all under Roman control.

Barnabas: Another interesting fact is that Barnabas was born here.

Paul: When Paul, Barnabas, and John Mark came to Cyprus from Antioch, they preached the gospel. The governor, Sergius Paulus, became a Christian.

John Mark: The sorcerer Elymas tried to win the governor back to paganism. But when Paul confronted him, Elymas was struck with blindness for his evil.

Barnabas: Paul, Barnabas, and John Mark traveled from Cyprus to Perga.

City 3—Perga

Paul, Barnabas, and John Mark walk to the person with the Perga sign.

Perga: Perga is a city in present-day Turkey. It was part of a Roman province known as Galatia. Because it was a port city, Perga became very prosperous. Perga was considered a "cathedral city" to the Greek goddess, Artemis—also known as Diana, Apollo's twin sister.

Antioch 2: Say, we have a temple here for the god Apollo.

Perga: Yes, you do. There was a lot of pagan worship in this part of the world.

Barnabas: While Paul, Barnabas, and John Mark were here, John Mark decided to leave his friends and return to Jerusalem.

133

John Mark walks back past Antioch of Syria.

Paul: Paul lost faith in John Mark because he left. Later, when Barnabas wanted to take him along on the next journey, Paul refused. On future missionary trips, Paul took Silas while Barnabas went with John Mark.

Barnabas: Paul and Barnabas then traveled from Perga to Antioch of Pisidia.

City 4—Antioch of Pisidia

Paul and Barnabas walk to the person with the Antioch of Pisidia sign.

Antioch of Pisidia: Antioch of Pisidia is also located in Galatia. Antioch of Pisidia was named by the Syrian general Seleucus after his father, Antiochus.

Antioch of Syria 1: Didn't I just say that about Antioch of Syria?

Antioch of Pisidia: Yes, you did. I guess Seleucus really liked his father. Many Jews settled here over the years. Antioch of Pisidia was known as a center for Hellenism—Greek culture and religion.

Paul: Paul and Barnabas came to the synagogue and preached about the death and resurrection of Jesus. Many Jews were interested in this teaching.

Barnabas: But the Jewish leaders became jealous and had Paul and Barnabas tossed out. When they left, Paul and Barnabas shook the dust from their sandals and said, "We now turn to the Gentiles."

Paul: Paul and Barnabas traveled from Perga to Iconium.

City 5—Iconium

Paul and Barnabas walk to the person with the Iconium sign.

Iconium: Iconium is another city located in the province of Galatia. It was a thriving and prosperous city during the first century. Two Roman emperors liked Iconium a lot. Because of that, it became rich and famous.

Paul: Paul and Barnabas came here to preach. Their words and the miracles the Spirit allowed them to do turned many Jewish and Gentile hearts to Jesus.

Barnabas: But it also caused great opposition, and a plot was hatched to stone the missionaries.

Paul: When Paul and Barnabas found out about that, they fled to Lystra.

City 6—Lystra

Paul and Barnabas walk to the person with the Lystra sign.

Lystra: Lystra was an out-of-the-way town in the southern mountains of Galatia.

Barnabas: Are we still in Galatia?

Lystra: Yes, you are. In fact Paul's friend and companion Timothy came from Lystra.

Paul: Paul and Barnabas came to Lystra after the attempted stoning in Iconium. But Lystra did not prove to be a refuge.

Barnabas: When Paul and Barnabas preached about Jesus, the people of Lystra misunderstood and wanted to worship Paul and Barnabas. They shouted, "The gods have come down to us in human form!"

Paul: Paul and Barnabas convinced the people not to worship them, but people from Antioch and Iconium turned the crowd against Paul and Barnabas. They stoned Paul and left him for dead.

Barnabas: He wasn't dead, though, and the next day Paul and Barnabas traveled to Derbe.

City 7—Derbe

Paul and Barnabas walk to the person with the Derbe sign.

Derbe: Derbe is the easternmost city on Paul and Barnabas's missionary trip. Nobody knows much about Derbe. It is also located in Galatia.

Paul: Later, Paul wrote a letter to the people in Galatia. We know that letter as the Epistle to the Galatians.

Barnabas: When Paul and Barnabas preached the good news of Jesus in Derbe, a large number of people believed and a church was established.

Paul: Paul and Barnabas then returned to Lystra, Iconium, and Antioch of Syria and gave a report of all they had heard and seen.

This article originally appeared in *Reformed Worship* 74, Dec. 2004, pages 3–5, used by permission.

Appendix B

Picture Books

These are some of the books that we have used with children in our worship centers for children three years old through third grade. This list is certainly not exhaustive. It is included here to give examples of how different kinds of literature can be used to help children see that their faith impacts all aspects of their life and the world in which we all live.

Ajimera, Maya, and John D. Ivanko. *To Be a Kid*. Watertown, MA: Charlesbridge Publishing, 1999.
> Words and photographs from countries around the world show that children everywhere have many things in common. It's helpful in discussing that the church of Jesus Christ is all around the world.

Aliki. *My Hands*. New York: HarperCollins, 1990.
> The book describes hands and looks at all the things they can do. This can be used with young children to talk about how wonderfully we are made.

Bahr, Mary, and Karen A. Jerome. *If Nathan Were Here*. Grand Rapids: Eerdmans, 2000.
>This book can help children think about people who have died.

Bozutti-Jones, Mark Francisco. *God Created*. Minneapolis: Augsburg, 2003.
>This is a fun creation book.

Brown, Susan Taylor, and Garin Baker. *Can I Pray with My Eyes Open?* New York: Hyperion, 1999.
>This book provides an excellent discussion of prayer.

Carle, Eric. *From Head to Toe*. New York: HarperCollins, 1997.
>This book can be used with young children to explore how we are wonderfully made.

Carle, Eric. *The Tiny Seed*. Saxonville, MA: Picture Book Studio, 1987.
>Describing a flowering plant's life cycle through the seasons, it can be used with the parable of the sower or to help explain how God gives us life.

Carle, Eric. *The Very Hungry Caterpillar*. New York: Putnam and Grossett, 1987.
>This story about a caterpillar who eats and eats until he becomes a butterfly is useful in talking about how God gives us new life.

Carlstrom, Nancy White. *Does God Know How to Tie Shoes?* Grand Rapids: Eerdmans, 1993.
>A child's questions explore who God is and how he is real for children. The book reinforces the idea that God is always with us, wrapping his love around us "like the wings of a mother hen protecting her baby chicks."

Carlstrom, Nancy White. *How Does the Wind Walk?* New York: Macmillan, 1993.
>A little boy watches the wind through the four seasons of the year. This book can be used in connection with Pentecost and the coming of the Holy Spirit as a rushing wind.

Caswell, Helen. *God Must Like to Laugh*. Nashville: Abingdon, 1987.
  God created a wide variety of wonders in the animal world.

Caswell, Helen. *I Can Talk with God*. Nashville: Abingdon, 1989.
  This book is written simply to help a child think about talking to God in different circumstances.

Daly, Jude. *To Everything There Is a Season*. Grand Rapids: Eerdmans, 2006.
  The words of Ecclesiastes 3:1–8.

Fairbridge, Lynne, and Georgia Graham. *We Need a Moose: A Story about Prayer*. Wheaton: Victor, 1996.
  This is a good book for starting a discussion about how God answers prayer.

Fitch, Florence Mary, and Henri Sorensen. *A Book about God*. New York: Lothrop, Lee and Shepard, 1953.
  This is an old book, first published in 1953 (it has since been republished in 1999 by HarperCollins). The author explores what God's presence is like.

Fogle, Jeanne S. *Seasons of God's Love: The Church Year*. Philadelphia: Geneva Press, 1988.
  This book explains the liturgical calendar.

Fogle, Jeanne S. *Signs of God's Love: Baptism and Communion*. Philadelphia: Geneva Press, 1984.
  Baptism and communion are explained in a clear and understandable way.

Fogle, Jeanne S. *Symbols of God's Love: Codes and Passwords*. Philadelphia: Geneva Press, 1986.
  This is a book that explores many of the common symbols that Christians use.

Fox, Mem, and Julie Vivas. *Wilfrid Gordon McDonald Partridge*. Brooklyn: Kane/Miller, 1995.
  This is a wonderful story about how a small boy, Wilfrid, helps

an old woman, Miss Nancy, recover her memory. Wilfrid brings objects to Miss Nancy, and she tells him stories from her past about the objects. This use of objects to help memory can lead into a discussion of communion.

Garland, Sherry. *The Lotus Seed*. New York: Harcourt, Brace, 1993.
A young Vietnamese girl saves a lotus seed and carries it with her everywhere to remember a brave emperor and the homeland that she has to flee. This can remind us of the new life we can have in Christ—just like the seed that when planted grows and creates more seeds.

Gray, Nigel, and Philippe Dupasquier. *A Country Far Away*. New York: Orchard Books, 1988.
In this book, about an ordinary day in the life of two boys, the page is split with the top half showing the life of a child in Africa and the bottom half showing a boy's life in the United States.

Greene, Rhonda Gowler, and Anne Wilson. *The Beautiful World That God Made*. Grand Rapids: Eerdmans, 2002.
A retelling of the creation story.

Greissman, Annette, and David Erickson. *Gabriel, God and the Fuzzy Blanket*. Harrisburg, PA: Morehouse, 2000.
A young boy learns that God is always with him, even when he forgets his favorite blanket.

Grimes, Nikki, and Michael Bryant. *Come Sunday*. Grand Rapids: Eerdmans, 1996.
A young girl's experiences at church on Sunday are described, from the blue-haired ladies to peeking during prayer (looking for a miracle).

Grimes, Nikki, and Paul Morin. *At Break of Day*. Grand Rapids: Eerdmans, 1999.
This is a beautifully illustrated book about creation.

Halperin, Wendy Anderson. *Love Is* . . . New York: Simon and Schuster, 2001.

> A reflection on 1 Corinthians 13.

Halperin, Wendy Anderson. *Turn! Turn! Turn!* New York: Simon and Schuster, 2003.

> The book includes the music and a CD using the words from the 1961 song by Pete Seeger based on Ecclesiastes 3.

Hardy, LeAnne, and Janet Wilson. *So That's What God Is Like*. Grand Rapids: Kregel, 2004.

> A child asks his grandmother on the way home from church what God is like. They find that God is like a rock, shepherd, minister, hen, mother, and even the wind.

Hodgson, Mona, and Hallie Gillett. *How Did Bible Heroes Pray?* Grand Rapids: Kregel, 2004.

> This book depicts Bible characters praying, showing that modern children can pray the same way.

Hodgson, Mona Gansber, and Chris Sharp. *I Wonder Who Stretched the Giraffe's Neck*. St. Louis: Concordia, 1999.

> This book explores God's creativity in making the world.

Hudson, Cheryl Willis, and John-Francis Bourke. *Hands Can*. Cambridge, MA: Candlewick, 2003.

> This book looks at all the wonderful things young children can do with their hands.

Jonas, Ann. *Round Trip*. New York: Greenwillow, 1983.

> Read the book forward and then backward and upside down. This is a book that can be used to help us look at the world in new ways and see God in it.

Joosse, Barbara M., and Barbara Lavalle. *Mama, Do You Love Me?* San Francisco: Chronicle Books, 1991.

> A story set in the Arctic about parental love. This can be used to reflect on God's love for us.

Ladwig, Tim. *The Lord's Prayer*. Grand Rapids: Eerdmans, 2000.
An illustrated version of the Lord's Prayer.

Ladwig, Tim. *Psalm Twenty-Three*. Grand Rapids: Eerdmans, 1993.
A visual reflection on Psalm 23, using images from the inner city.

Lindbergh, Reeve, and Cathie Felstead. *The Circle of Days*. Cambridge, MA: Candlewick, 1998.
An adaptation in pictures of "Canticle of the Sun" by Saint Francis of Assisi, a hymn of praise showing how all creation praises God.

Lindbergh, Reeve, and Holly Meade. *On Morning Wings*. Cambridge, MA: Candlewick, 2002.
An adaptation of Psalm 139.

Lucado, Max. *Just in Case You Ever Wonder*. Dallas: Word, 1992.
This book is a celebration of our love and God's love for our children, even as they grow and change.

MacLachlan, Patricia. *All the Places to Love*. New York: HarperCollins, 1994.
A young boy describes the favorite places that he shares with his family on his grandparents' farm and in the nearby countryside. This book can be used to begin a discussion of covenant and of passing on the faith from generation to generation.

Martin, Bill Jr., Michael Sampson, and Cathie Felstead. *Adam, Adam, What Do You See?* Nashville: Tommy Nelson, 2000.
This book uses the pattern of "Brown Bear, Brown Bear, what do you see?" using biblical characters.

McBratney, Sam, and Anita Jeram. *Guess How Much I Love You*. Cambridge, MA: Candlewick, 1995.
A mother hare answers her baby hare's question about love.

McKee, David. *Elmer*. New York: Lothrop, Lee, and Shepard Books, 1968.
All the elephants of the jungle were gray except Elmer, who was

a patchwork of brilliant colors. Elmer made them laugh with his jokes. One day he got tired of being different and painted himself gray. The other elephants missed Elmer, his colors, and his humor. This book can be used to begin a discussion of how we are all valued for who we are.

Ramshaw, Gail. *Every Day and Sunday, Too.* Minneapolis: Augsburg Fortress, 1996.
    A book that shows the common parts of Christian worship.

Rock, Lois. *Before the Stars Were Made.* Oxford: Lion, 1997.
    This wonderfully written book helps children see how the stories of creation, Christmas, and Easter all weave together.

Ryder, Joanne. *My Father's Hands.* New York: Morrow, 1994.
    A father shows his daughter plants and insects in their garden. The book can be used to remind children that God has the whole world in his hands.

Sasso, Sandy Eisenberg. *In God's Name.* Woodstock, VT: Jewish Lights, 1994.
    This book explores the different names for God, like Creator of Light and Shepherd.

Wangerin, Walter Jr., and Gerardo Suzán. *Water, Come Down! The Day You Were Baptized.* Minneapolis: Augsburg Fortress, 1999.
    A beautifully written celebration of infant baptism.

Weeks, Sarah, and David Diaz. *Angel Face.* New York: Athenaeum, 2002.
    A small boy wanders away from his mother, and she enlists the help of an old crow to find him. The mother describes the child as so beautiful that the crow almost flies by a plain-looking child. When the crow figures out that this is the child he is looking for, he realizes that every child is beautiful in his mother's eyes. This book can be used to think about how God views us.

Wick, Walter. *A Drop of Water: A Book of Science and Wonder.* New York: Scholastic, 1997.
Wonderful pictures and text explore water and provide a good way to talk about the wonder of God's world.

Wildsmith, Brian. *Animal Shapes.* Oxford: Oxford University Press, 1981.
This brightly illustrated animal book can be used with young children when talking about creation.

Wildsmith, Brian. *Brian Wildsmith's Birds.* Oxford: Oxford University Press, 1967.
This brightly illustrated animal book can be used with young children when talking about creation.

Wildsmith, Brian. *Brian Wildsmith's Fishes.* Oxford: Oxford University Press, 1968.
This brightly illustrated animal book can be used with young children when talking about creation.

Ziefert, Harriet, and Todd McKie. *First He Made the Sun.* New York: Putnam, 2000.
An illustrated version of the creation story.

Notes

Chapter 1 Three-Dimensional Faith

1. See Marva J. Dawn, *Is It a Lost Cause? Having the Heart of God for the Church's Children* (Grand Rapids: Eerdmans, 1997), 59.

2. Dan Kimball also mentions this as one of the reasons for the importance of rethinking worship for postmodern young people in *The Emerging Church* (Grand Rapids: Zondervan, 2003).

3. Tony Campolo tells this about Karl Barth in *Let Me Tell You a Story* (Dallas: Word, 2000), 22–23.

Chapter 2 The Church as Community

1. A further discussion of *mishpahah* can be found in Marvin Wilson's book *Our Father Abraham: Jewish Roots of the Christian Faith* (Grand Rapids: Eerdmans, 1989), 188, 210.

2. For another interesting discussion of the complex family structure in ancient Israel, see Daniel Block's chapter, "Marriage and Family in Ancient Israel," in *Marriage and Family in the Biblical World*, ed. Ken M. Campbell (Downers Grove, IL: InterVarsity, 2003), 33–102.

3. There are a number of times that the phrase "my father's house" is used in the Gospels in addition to the story of Jesus in the temple. Jesus refers to the temple again as "my father's house" in John 2 when he clears the temple. In the story of the rich man and Lazarus in Luke 16:19–31, when the rich man asks Abraham to send a messenger to tell his brothers about

what has happened, he asks Abraham to send him to "my father's house." Finally, Jesus references this concept and the idea that the house was more like a compound when he tells his disciples: "In my Father's house are many rooms" (John 14:2).

4. This may be what God is referring to in Exodus 20:5 where he says the third and fourth generation will be punished for the sin of the fathers.

5. Block, "Marriage and Family in Ancient Israel," 47.

6. Wilson, *Our Father Abraham*, 211.

7. Commission for Children at Risk, *Hardwired to Connect: The New Scientific Case for Authoritative Communities* (New York: Institute for American Values, 2003), 9.

8. Ibid., 14.

9. See Wilson, *Our Father Abraham*, 298, for a discussion of the Hebrew system of education.

10. I don't want to give the impression that life was a bed of roses for children in the first century. As we'll see later, children had very low status in society and were sometimes mistreated and ignored. There are some things about the first-century family and community structure, however, from which we can learn.

11. I'll say more about how our worship centers are structured in chapter 7.

12. We chose to interview parents rather than ask them just to come in and talk about their faith, since preparing a presentation can be intimidating for some, and we wanted this to be more of a conversation about faith than a stiff presentation.

13. Debra Reinstra, *So Much More: An Invitation to Christian Spirituality* (San Francisco: Jossey-Bass, 2005), 197.

14. Donald Posterski, *Friendship: A Window on Ministry to Youth* (Scarborough, Ontario, Canada: Project Teen Canada, 1986), 89–90.

Chapter 3 Jesus Values Children

1. The same story is also told in Mark 5.

2. Many biblical scholars believe that Matthew and Luke used Mark's Gospel as source material in writing their accounts of the life and teachings of Jesus for their particular audiences. These three Gospels, then, are called the *Synoptic* Gospels because they often, but not always, cover the same events in very similar ways. Gordon Fee and Douglas Stuart have a good discussion of this in *How to Read the Bible for All Its Worth*, 3rd ed. (Grand Rapids: Zondervan, 2003).

3. This story is also found in Matthew 18:1–5 and Luke 9:46–48.

4. Wilson, *Our Father Abraham*, 136.

5. Ibid.

6. See Ray VanderLaan and Judith Markham, *Echoes of His Presence* (Grand Rapids: Zondervan, 1996), for more information on this.

7. Judith Gundry-Volf, "The Least and the Greatest: Children in the New Testament," in *The Child in Christian Thought*, ed. Marcia Bunge (Grand Rapids: Eerdmans, 2001), 32.

8. Ibid., 32–33.

9. Parables were another example of the rabbinic style. For more information see Roy B. Zuck, *Teaching as Jesus Taught* (Grand Rapids: Baker, 1995).

10. The New International Version uses the word "welcomes." Some other versions use the word "receives."

11. The other incident is the one in which Jesus removes the money changers from the temple. This is shown in Matt. 21:12–13; Mark 11:15–17; and Luke 19:45–46. While the Gospel writers never actually state that Jesus is angry, his tone and actions certainly suggest it!

12. Arthur S. Peake, ed., *A Commentary on the Bible* (London: T. C. and E. C. Jack, 1920), 693.

13. This story is also found in Matthew 19:13–15 and in Luke 18:15–17.

14. James L. Mays, ed., *Harper Bible Commentary* (San Francisco: HarperSanFrancisco, 1988), 992.

15. Albert Barnes, *Notes on the New Testament: Matthew and Mark* (Grand Rapids: Baker, 1949), 367–68.

16. Walter Roehrs and Martin Franzmann, *Concordia Self-Study Commentary* (St. Louis: Concordia Publishing, 1979), 33.

17. http://www.barna.org/FlexPage.aspx?Page=Topic&TopicID=18 (July 30, 2004).

Chapter 4 Dwelling in the Mysteries

1. Anne Lamott, *Plan B: Further Thoughts on Faith* (New York: Riverhead Books, 2005), 256–57.

2. Craig Dykstra has an interesting and important critique of Fowler's theory in Craig Dykstra and Sharon Parks, eds., *Faith Development and Fowler* (Birmingham, AL: Religious Education Press, 1981).

3. James Fowler, *Stages of Faith* (San Francisco: Harper and Row), 1981.

4. While these concepts are generally agreed on by almost all theorists, the wording for this particular listing of them comes from Anita Woolfolk, *Educational Psychology*, 9th ed. (Boston: Allyn and Bacon, 2004), 24.

5. Not all adults continue to develop, but the potential is there most of the time.

6. As with all the other faith stages, this information is presented in a comprehensive way in Fowler's book *Stages of Faith*.

7. Charles R. McCollough, *Heads of Heaven, Feet of Clay* (New York: Pilgrim Press, 1983), 32.

8. Mary Pipher, *Reviving Ophelia: Saving the Selves of Adolescent Girls* (New York: Ballantine, 1994), 71.

9. John Westerhoff is the other person who has written most extensively about faith development and, while there are some differences between his theory and James Fowler's, they both agree on this point. See John H. Westerhoff, *Bringing Up Children in the Christian Faith* (Minneapolis: Winston, 1980).

10. The way McLaren's book is constructed, the story of Kerry is not given as a factual story but as part of a fictional discussion. It is clear, though, that McLaren is basing his story on a real situation.

11. Brian D. McLaren, *The Story We Find Ourselves In: Further Adventures of a New Kind of Christian* (San Francisco: Jossey-Bass, 2003), 7.

Chapter 5 The Power of Story

1. Francis Schaeffer spends all of chapter 1 in his book *Joshua and the Flow of Biblical History* (Downers Grove, IL: InterVarsity, 1975) discussing this issue and other ways that Joshua was prepared for leadership.

2. Fee and Stuart, in *How to Read the Bible for All Its Worth*, page 21, write that the Bible has "eternal relevance" but also "historical particularity."

3. Many of the stories in the Old and the New Testaments were told orally for years before they were written down.

4. Catherine Stonehouse, *Joining Children on the Spiritual Journey: Nurturing a Life of Faith* (Grand Rapids: Baker, 1998), 161.

5. Robert Coles, *The Spiritual Life of Children* (Boston: Houghton Mifflin, 1990), 121.

6. Jerome Berryman, *Godly Play* (Minneapolis: Augsburg, 1991), 66–67.

7. Note that my friend told this story to make a point. We assume that Bible stories are also told to make a point, but we don't always know what God's point is. I prefer to think that there are often many things that we can learn from each story and that God can use the same story to teach a variety of lessons.

8. Berryman, *Godly Play*, 69.

Chapter 6 Obedience and Faith

1. Kohlberg published his theory in *The Psychology of Moral Development* (New York: Harper and Row, 1984). This work is reported and critiqued in a number of places, including Fowler, *Stages of Faith*; Perry G. Downs, *Teaching for Spiritual Growth: An Introduction to Christian Spirituality* (Grand Rapids: Zondervan, 1994); and Stonehouse, *Joining Children on the Spiritual Journey.*

2. Remember, the ages given in developmental theories like this are only a general indication of the age at which many people are in this stage.

3. This is when children are in the *concrete operational* stage of cognitive development. You can read more about this in John L. Phillips Jr., *The Origins of Intellect: Piaget's Theory* (San Francisco: W. H. Freeman, 1969), 63.

4. I'm most certainly not advocating an "anything goes" policy for children! Just because they operate from self-interest doesn't mean we can't make it in their self-interest to do the right things. I'm merely pointing out what is behind some of their decisions.

5. Downs, *Teaching for Spiritual Growth*, 17–19.

6. Bonnie J. Miller-McLemore goes into great detail concerning the different ways of looking at children and sin in chapter 3 of her book, *Let the Children Come: Reimagining Childhood from a Christian Perspective* (San Francisco: Jossey-Bass, 2003).

7. Fowler, *Stages of Faith*, 134.

8. Sue Miller and David Staal, *Making Your Children's Ministry the Best Hour of Every Kid's Week* (Grand Rapids: Zondervan, 2004), 73.

9. Ibid., 72.

10. Ibid., 74.

11. Gretchen Wolff Pritchard, *Offering the Gospel to Children* (Cambridge, MA: Cowley, 1992), 21.

12. Fee and Stuart, *How to Read the Bible for All Its Worth*, 90; italics in the original.

13. Ibid., 103.

14. Dennis Hoekstra, *Christian Education through Religious Studies* (Grand Rapids: Calvin College, 1985). The electronic version of the monograph *Christian Education Through Religious Studies* can be found at http://www.calvin.edu/academic/education/news/publications/monoweb/hoekstra.htm.

15. Endings can be hard for storytellers. Often when my students tell stories, they come to an awkward conclusion. As you work on your storytelling, develop ways that are comfortable for you to close your story.

Chapter 7 Worship

1. Mark DeVries, *Family-Based Youth Ministry* (Downers Grove, IL: InterVarsity, 1994), 21.

2. A brief history of this shift can be found in "Disconnected Rituals," a chapter in Todd Johnson, ed., *The Conviction of Things Not Seen: Worship and Ministry in the 21st Century* (Grand Rapids: Brazos Press, 2002).

3. There is a very nice introduction to the topics of exegesis (determining the original meaning of a text) and hermeneutics (applying that text to today) in the first chapter of Fee and Stuart, *How to Read the Bible for All Its Worth.*

4. See my notes on developmental theories on pages 51–53.

5. There are other more recent theories of cognitive development that extend development into adulthood, but Piaget's work is still seen as a great place to start for understanding the topic.

6. Sonja M. Stewart and Jerome W. Berryman, *Young Children and Worship* (Louisville: Westminster John Knox, 1989), 13.

7. Karen Wilk, "Is Our Worship R-Rated?" *CRC Source* 8, no. 2 (2003), 5.

8. Note that this argument for having separate worship for children is based on developmental ability not preference. This argument doesn't work for those who want separate teen worship. While some churches might want to have special teen worship services to give teens more ownership of the worship service, I think the whole congregation is better served by having teens worship with and have a part in leading worship for the entire congregation.

9. Carolyn C. Brown, *Gateways to Worship* (Nashville: Abingdon Press, 1989); *You Can Preach to the Kids Too: Designing Sermons for Adults and Children* (Nashville: Abingdon Press, 1997). Debbie Hough and Mary E. Speedy, *Children in the Sanctuary Study Guide* (Louisville, KY: Church Leader Support, Presbyterian Church U.S.A., 2002). Karen Wilk, ed., *Together All God's People: Integrating Children and Youth into the Life of the Church* (Grand Rapids: Faith Alive Christian Resources, 2005). Howard VanderWell, ed., *The Church of All Ages: Generations Worshiping Together* (Herndon, VA: Alban Institute, 2008).

10. Craig R. Dykstra, *Vision and Character: A Christian Educator's Alternative to Kohlberg* (New York: Paulist Press, 1981), 106.

Chapter 8 Creating a Child-Friendly Culture

1. Laura Keeley and I have published a number of our Christmas programs though Faith Alive Christian Resources. They can be found at www

.faithaliveresources.org. Titles include *Born for You and Me, Manger King, The Very Best Gift of All, Promises Promises, I've Got Mail,* and *Not Forgotten.*

2. Barbara Robinson's book *The Best Christmas Pageant Ever* (New York: HarperCollins, 1972) tells the story of a little girl who expected to get the role of Mary in the Christmas play because that was the best role. She is disappointed that one of the neighborhood children, someone who doesn't even come to church all the time, gets the part. This is a wonderful book that really lets you see inside the head of a child as she prepares for the church Christmas program. Aside from being a fun book to read, it gives great insight into the trials of putting on one of these programs!

3. Carolyn C. Brown, *Sharing the Easter Faith with Children* (Nashville: Abingdon, 2006), 25.

4. George Barna, *Transforming Children into Spiritual Champions* (Ventura, CA: Gospel Light Publications, 2003), 24.

5. Reading the blogs (web logs) of the kids in your church and in your family is a great way to have your finger on the pulse of what they're thinking and feeling. I figure that anything they post on the Internet is fair game for my reading. If they know I'm reading what they write, it reminds them that their thoughts are posted in a place where many people can read them and it helps keep them from posting things that are too personal.

Bibliography

Barna, George. *The Barna Group*. The Barna Group, LTD. 13 July 2006 http://www.barna.org/FlexPage.aspx?Page=Topic&TopicID=18.

Barnes, Albert. *Notes on the New Testament: Matthew and Mark*. Grand Rapids: Baker, 1949.

Berryman, Jerome W. *Godly Play*. Minneapolis: Augsburg, 1991.

Brown, Carolyn C. *Sharing the Easter Faith with Children*. Nashville: Abingdon, 2006.

Campbell, Ken M., ed. *Marriage and Family in the Biblical World*. Downers Grove, IL: InterVarsity, 2003.

Campolo, Tony. *Let Me Tell You a Story*. Dallas: Word, 2000.

Coles, Robert. *The Spiritual Life of Children*. Boston: Houghton Mifflin, 1990.

Commission for Children at Risk. *Hardwired to Connect: The New Scientific Case for Authoritative Communities*. New York: Institute for American Values, 2003.

Dawn, Marva J. *Is It a Lost Cause? Having the Heart of God for the Church's Children*. Grand Rapids: Eerdmans, 1997.

DeVries, Mark. *Family-Based Youth Ministry*. Downers Grove, IL: InterVarsity, 1994.

Downs, Perry G. *Teaching for Spiritual Growth: An Introduction to Christian Spirituality*. Grand Rapids: Zondervan, 1994.

Dykstra, Craig R. *Vision and Character: A Christian Educator's Alternative to Kohlberg*. New York: Paulist Press, 1981.

Dykstra, Craig, and Sharon Parks, eds. *Faith Development and Fowler*. Birmingham, AL: Religious Education Press, 1986.

Fee, Gordon D., and Douglas Stuart. *How to Read the Bible for All Its Worth*. 3rd ed. Grand Rapids: Zondervan, 2003.

Fowler, James. *Stages of Faith*. San Francisco: Harper and Row, 1981.

Garland, Sherry, and Tatsuro Kiuchi. *The Lotus Seed*. San Diego: Harcourt, Brace, 1993.

Gundry-Volf, Judith. "The Least and the Greatest: Children in the New Testament." In *The Child in Christian Thought*, ed. Marcia J. Bunge. Grand Rapids: Eerdmans, 2001.

Hoekstra, Dennis. *Christian Education through Religious Studies*. Grand Rapids: Calvin College, 1985.

Johnson, Todd E. "Disconnected Rituals." In *The Conviction of Things Not Seen: Worship and Ministry in the 21st Century*, ed. Todd E. Johnson. Grand Rapids: Brazos, 2002.

Kimball, Dan. *The Emerging Church*. Grand Rapids: Zondervan, 2003.

Ladwig, Tim. *Psalm Twenty-Three*. Grand Rapids: Eerdmans, 1993.

Lamott, Anne. *Plan B: Further Thoughts on Faith*. New York: Riverhead Books, 2005.

MacLachlan, Patricia, and Michael Wimmer. *All the Places to Love*. New York: HarperCollins, 1994.

Mays, James L., ed. *Harper Bible Commentary*. San Francisco: HarperSanFrancisco, 1988.

McCollough, Charles R. *Heads of Heaven, Feet of Clay*. New York: Pilgrim Press, 1983.

McLaren, Brian D. *The Story We Find Ourselves In: Further Adventures of a New Kind of Christian*. San Francisco: Jossey-Bass, 2003.

Miller, Sue, and David Staal. *Making Your Children's Ministry the Best Hour of Every Kid's Week*. Grand Rapids: Zondervan, 2004.

Miller-McLemore, Bonnie J. *Let the Children Come: Reimagining Childhood from a Christian Perspective*. San Francisco: Jossey-Bass, 2003.

Peake, Arthur S., ed. *A Commentary on the Bible*. London: T. C. and E. C. Jack, 1920.

Phillips, John L., Jr. *The Origins of Intellect: Piaget's Theory*. San Francisco: W. H. Freeman, 1969.

Pipher, Mary. *Reviving Ophelia: Saving the Selves of Adolescent Girls*. New York: Ballantine, 1994.

Posterski, Donald C. *Friendship: A Window on Ministry to Youth*. Scarborough, Ontario, Canada: Project Teen Canada, 1986.

Pritchard, Gretchen Wolff. *Offering the Gospel to Children*. Cambridge, MA: Cowley, 1992.

Reinstra, Debra. *So Much More: An Invitation to Christian Spirituality*. San Francisco: Jossey-Bass, 2005.

Robinson, Barbara. *The Best Christmas Pageant Ever*. New York: HarperCollins, 1972.

Roehrs, Walter, and Martin Franzmann. *Concordia Self-Study Commentary*. St. Louis: Concordia, 1979.

Schaeffer, Francis A. *Joshua and the Flow of Biblical History*. Downers Grove, IL: InterVarsity Press, 1975.

Stewart, Sonja M., and Jerome W. Berryman. *Young Children and Worship*. Louisville: Westminster John Knox, 1989.

Stonehouse, Catherine, *Joining Children on the Spiritual Journey: Nurturing a Life of Faith*. Grand Rapids: Baker, 1998.

VanderLaan, Ray, and Judith Markham. *Echoes of His Presence*. Grand Rapids: Zondervan, 1996.

Warren, Rick. *The Purpose Driven Life.* Grand Rapids: Zondervan, 2002.

Westerhoff, John H. *Bringing Up Children in the Christian Faith.* Minneapolis: Winston, 1980.

Wilk, Karen. "Is Our Worship R-Rated?" *CRC Source* 8, no. 2 (2003).

Wilson, Marvin R. *Our Father Abraham: Jewish Roots of the Christian Faith.* Grand Rapids: Eerdmans, 1989.

Woolfolk, Anita. *Educational Psychology.* 9th ed. Boston: Allyn and Bacon, 2004.

Zuck, Roy B. *Teaching as Jesus Taught.* Grand Rapids: Baker, 1995.

Robert Keeley is a professor of education at Calvin College in Grand Rapids, Michigan, and codirector with his wife, Laura, of children's ministries at Fourteenth Street Christian Reformed Church in Holland, Michigan.